Lucas Malet, Paul Hardy

Little Peter

A Christmas Morality for Children of Any Age

Lucas Malet, Paul Hardy

Little Peter
A Christmas Morality for Children of Any Age

ISBN/EAN: 9783337379865

Printed in Europe, USA, Canada, Australia, Japan

Cover: Foto ©Lupo / pixelio.de

More available books at **www.hansebooks.com**

A
CHRISTMAS MORALITY

"Remember my ears are so quick I can hear the grass grow."

Frontispiece.

LITTLE PETER

A CHRISTMAS MORALITY

FOR CHILDREN OF ANY AGE

BY LUCAS MALET

AUTHOR OF 'COLONEL ENDERBY'S WIFE' ETC.

WITH NUMEROUS ILLUSTRATIONS BY PAUL HARDY

LONDON
KEGAN PAUL, TRENCH, & CO., 1 PATERNOSTER SQUARE
1888

TO

CECILY

IN TOKEN OF AFFECTION

TOWARDS HERSELF, HER MOTHER, AND HER STATELY HOME

THIS LITTLE STORY IS DEDICATED

BY

HER OBEDIENT SERVANT

LUCAS MALET

CONTENTS.

CHAPTER		PAGE
I.	Which deals with the opinions of a Cat, and the sorrows of a Charcoal-burner	1
II.	Which introduces the Reader to an Admirer of the Ancient Romans	19
III.	Which improves our acquaintance with the Grasshopper-man	36
IV.	Which leaves some at Home, and takes some to Church	50
V.	Which is both Social and Religious	68
VI.	Which attempts to show why the Skies fall	84
VII.	Which describes a pleasant Dinner Party, and an unpleasant Walk	95

CONTENTS

CHAPTER		PAGE
VIII.	WHICH PROVES THAT EVEN PHILOSOPHIC POLITICIANS MAY HAVE TO ADMIT THEMSELVES IN THE WRONG	115
IX.	WHICH IS VERY SHORT BECAUSE, IN SOME WAYS, IT IS RATHER SAD	132
X.	WHICH ENDS THE STORY	143

ILLUSTRATIONS.

'REMEMBER MY EARS ARE SO QUICK I CAN HEAR THE GRASS GROW'.		*Frontispiece*
'WHAT WILL HAPPEN? PLEASE TELL ME'.	*To face p.*	10
'GO TO BED WHEN YOU ARE TOLD'	,,	34
'YOU ALL DESPISE ME'	,,	66
GOING TO CHURCH	,,	72
LOST	,,	110
WAITING	,,	120
FOUND	,,	138
THE CHARCOAL-BURNER VISITS LITTLE PETER	,,	150

LITTLE PETER.

CHAPTER I.

WHICH DEALS WITH THE OPINIONS OF A CAT,
AND THE SORROWS OF A CHARCOAL BURNER.

THE pine forest is a wonderful place. The pine-trees stand in ranks like the soldiers of some vast army, side by side, mile after mile, in companies and regiments and battalions, all clothed in a sober uniform of green and grey. But they are unlike soldiers in this, that they are of all ages and sizes; some so small that the rabbits easily jump over them in their play, and some so tall and stately that the fall of them is like the falling of a high tower. And the pine-trees are put to many different uses. They are made into masts for the gallant ships that sail out and away to distant ports across the great ocean. Others are sawn into planks, and used for the building of sheds; for the rafters and flooring, and clap-boards and woodwork of our houses; for railway-sleepers, and scaffoldings, and hoardings. Others are polished and fashioned into articles of furniture. Turpentine comes from them, which the artist uses with his colours, and the doctor in his medicines; which is used, too, in the cleaning of stuffs and in a hundred different ways. While the pine-cones, and broken branches and waste wood, make bright crackling fires by which to warm ourselves on a winter's day.

But there is something more than just this I should like you to think about in connection with the pine forest; for it, like everything else that is fair and noble in nature, has a strange and precious secret of its own.

You may learn the many uses of the trees in your school books, when men have cut them down or grubbed them up, or poked holes in their poor sides to let the turpentine run out. But you can only learn the secret of the forest itself by listening humbly and reverently for it to speak to you. For Nature is a very great lady, grander and more magnificent than all the queens who have lived in sumptuous palaces and reigned over famous kingdoms since the world began; and though she will be very kind and gracious to children who come and ask her questions modestly and prettily, and will show them the most lovely sights and tell them the most delicious fairy tales that ever were seen or heard, she makes very short work with conceited and impudent persons. She covers their eyes and stops their ears, so that they can never see her wonderful treasures or hear her charming stories, but live, all their lives long, shut up in the dark fusty cupboard of their own ignorance, and stupid self-love, and self-satisfaction, thinking they know all about everything as well as if they had made it themselves, when they do not really know anything at all. And because you and I dislike fusty cupboards, and because we want to know anything and everything that Nature is condescending enough to teach us, we will listen, to begin with, to what the pine forest has to tell.

When the rough winds are up and at play, and the pine-trees shout and sing together in a mighty chorus, while the hoarse voice of them is like the roar of the sea upon a rocky coast, then you may learn the secret of the forest. It sings first of the winged seed; and then of the birth of the tiny tree; of sunrise and sunset, and the tranquil warmth of noon-day, and of the soft, refreshing rain, and the kindly, nourishing earth, and of the white moon-light, and pale, moist garments of the mist, all helping the tree to grow up tall and straight, to strike root deep and spread wide its green branches. It sings, too, of the biting frost, and the still, dumb snow, and the hurrying storm, all trying and testing the tree, to prove if it can stand firm and show a brave face in time of danger and trouble. Then it sings of the happy spring-time, when the forest is girdled about with a band of flowers; while the birds build and call to each other among the high branches; and the squirrel helps his wife to make her snug nest for the little, brown squirrel-babies that are to be; and the dormice wake up from their long winter sleep, and sit in the sunshine and comb their whiskers with their dainty, little paws. And then the forest sings of man—how he comes with axe and saw, and hammer and iron wedges, and lays low the tallest of its children, and binds them with ropes and chains, and hauls them away to be his bond-servants and slaves. And, last of all, it sings slowly and very gently of old age and decay and death; of the seed that falls on hard, dry places and never springs up; of the tree that is broken by the tempest or scathed by the lightning flash, and stands bare and barren and unsightly; sings how, in the end, all things shrink and crumble, and how the dust of them returns and is mingled with the fruitful soil from which at first they came.

This is the song of the pine forest, and from it you may learn this lesson: that the life of the tree and of beast and bird are subject to the same three great laws as the life of man—the law of growth, of obedience, and of self-sacrifice. And perhaps, when you are older, if you take care to avoid that spirit of conceit and impudence which, as we have already said, gets people into such trouble with Nature, you may come to see that these three laws are after all but one, bound for ever together by the golden cord of love.

Once upon a time, just on the edge of the pine forest, there lived a little boy. He lived in a big, brown, wooden house, with overhanging eaves and a very deep roof to it, which swept down from the high middle gable like the wings of a hen covering her chickens. The wood-sheds, and hay-barn, and the stable where the brown-eyed, sweet-breathed cows lay at night, and the clean, cool dairy, and the cheese-room with its heavy presses were all under this same wide sheltering roof. Before the house a meadow of rich grass stretched down to a stream, that hurried along over rocky limestone ledges, or slipped away over flat sandy places where you might see the little fishes playing at hide-and-seek or puss in the corner among the bright pebbles at the bottom. While on the shallow, marshy puddles by the stream side, where the forget-me-not and brook-lime and rushes grow, the water-spiders would dance quadrilles and jigs and reels all day long in the sunshine, and the frogs would croak by hundreds in the still spring evenings, when the sunset was red behind the pine-trees to the west. And in this pleasant place little Peter lived, as I say, once upon a time, with his father and mother, and his two brothers, and Eliza the servant-maid, and Gustavus the cowherd.

He was the youngest of the children by a number of years, and was such a small fellow that Susan Lepage, his mother, could make him quite a smart blouse and pair of trousers out of Antony's cast-off garments, even when all the patches and thin places had been cut out. He had a black, curly head, and very round eyes—for many things surprised him, and surprise makes the eyes grow round as everybody knows—and a dear, little, red mouth, that was sweet to kiss, and nice, fat cheeks, which began to look rather cold and blue, by the way, as he stood on the threshold one evening about Christmas time, with Cincinnatus, the old, tabby tom-cat, under his arm. He was waiting for his brother Antony to come home from the neighbouring market-town of Nullepart. It was growing dusk, yet the sky was very clear. The sound of the wind in the pine branches and of the chattering stream was strange in the frosty evening air; so that little Peter felt rather creepy, as the saying is, and held on very tight to Cincinnatus for fear of—he didn't quite know what.

'Come in, little man, come in,' cried his mother, as she moved to and fro in the ruddy firelight, helping Eliza to get ready the supper. 'You will be frozen standing there outside; and we shall be frozen, too, sitting here with the door open. Antony will get home none the quicker for your watching. That which is looked for hardest, they say, comes last.'

But Peter only hugged Cincinnatus a little closer—thereby making that long-suffering animal kick spasmodically with his hind legs, as a rabbit does when you hold it up by the ears—and looked more earnestly than ever down the forest path into the dimness of the pines.

Just then John Paqualin, the charcoal-burner, came up to the open door, with a couple of empty sacks across his shoulders. Now the charcoal-burner was a great friend of little Peter's, though he was a queer figure to look at. For his red hair hung in wild locks down over his shoulders, and his eyes glowed red too—as red as his own smouldering charcoal fires—and his back was bent and crooked; while his legs were so inordinately long and thin, that all the naughty little boys in Nullepart, when he went down there to sell his sacks of charcoal, used to run after him up the street, shouting:—

'Hurrah, hurrah! here's the grasshopper man again! Hey, ho! grasshopper, give us a tune—haven't you brought your fiddle?'

But when Paqualin got annoyed, as he sometimes did, and turned round upon them with his glowing eyes, they would all scuttle away as hard as their legs could carry them. For, like a good many other people, they were particularly courageous when they could only see the enemy's back. You may be sure our little Peter never called the charcoal-burner by any offensive names, and therefore, having a good conscience, had no cause to be afraid of him.

'Eh! but what is this?' he cried, in his high cracked voice as he flung down the sacks, and stood by the little lad in the doorway. 'Remember my ears are so quick I can hear the grass grow. Just now I heard the best mother in the world call her little boy to go indoors, and here he stands still on the threshold. If you do not go in do you know what will happen, eh?'

'No; what will happen? Please tell me,' said Peter.

The charcoal-burner stretched out one long arm and pointed away into the forest, and sunk his voice to a whisper:—

'WHAT WILL HAPPEN? PLEASE TELL ME.'

Page 10.

'The old, grey she-wolf will assuredly come pit-a-pat, pit-a-pat over the moss and the stones, pit-a-pat over the pine-needles and the fallen twigs and branches, pit-a-pat out of the wood, and—snap!—like that, catch your poor Cincinnatus by the tail and carry him off to make into soup for her little ones. Picture to yourself poor Cincinnatus in the wolf's great, black, steaming soup-pot, and all the wolf-cubs with their wicked, little mouths wide open, sitting round, with their wooden spoons in their hands, all ready to begin.'

Peter retreated hastily into the kitchen, cat and all, and took up his stand rather close to his mother.

'Is it true, mother?' he said. 'But where do the wolves buy their wooden spoons, do you think —in the shop at Nullepart?'

'Nay, how should I know?' said Susan Lepage, as she stooped down and kissed the child, and then looking up kindly nodded to the charcoal-burner. 'You must ask the old she-wolf herself if you want to know where she buys her spoons, and her soup pot too for that matter. She is no friend of mine, little one.'

After a moment's pause, she added :—

'You will stay to supper, John Paqualin? My husband and sons will be in soon, and there is plenty for all, thank God. You will be welcome.'

But Paqualin shook his head, and the light died away in those strange eyes of his.

'Welcome?' he said. 'The pretty, false word has little meaning for me. And yet perhaps in your mouth it is honest, Susan Lepage, for you are gentle and merciful as a saint in heaven, and the child, here, takes after you. But, for the rest, who welcomes a mad, mis-shapen, half-finished creature on whom Nature herself has had no mercy? Master Lepage will come in hungry. Will he like to have his stomach turned by the sight of the hump-backed charcoal-burner? No, no, I go home to my hut. Good-night, little Peter. I will tell the grey wolf to look elsewhere for her supper.—Ah! I see wonderful things though sometimes, for all that I live alone and in squalor. The red fire and the white moon tell me stories, turn by turn, all the night through.'

And with that he swung the empty sacks across his back again and shambled away into the growing darkness.

'A good riddance,' muttered Eliza, as she set the cheese on the table. 'It is an absolute indignity to ask a respectable servant to wait at table on a wild animal like that.'

But Susan Lepage sighed as she turned from the doorway.

'Poor, unhappy one,' she said. 'God gave thee thy fair soul, but who gave thee thy ungainly body?'

Then she reproved Eliza for her conduct in various matters which had nothing in the world to do with her remarks upon the charcoal-burner. Even the best of women are not always quite logical.

Meanwhile little Peter had sat down on his stool by the fire. For a little while he sat very still, for he was thinking over the visit of his friend John Paqualin. He felt rather unhappy about him, he could not quite have said why. But when we are children it is not easy to think of any one person or one thing for long together. There are such lots of things to think about, that one chases another out of our heads very quickly. And so Peter soon gave up puzzling himself about the charcoal-burner, and began counting the sparks as they flew out of the blazing, crackling, pine logs up the wide chimney.

Unfortunately, however, he was not a great arithmetician; and though he began over and over again at plain one, two, three, he always got wrong among the fifteens and sixteens; and never succeeded in counting up to twenty at all. Nothing is more tedious than making frequent mistakes. So he got off his stool, and began hopping from one stone quarry in the kitchen floor to the next. Suddenly he became entangled in Eliza's full petticoats—she was whirling them about a good deal, it is true, being in rather a bad temper—and nearly tumbled down on his poor, little nose.

'Bless the child, what possesses him?' cried Eliza.

Peter retired to his stool again, in a hurry; and after thinking for a minute pulled a long bit of string, with a cross-bar of stick at the end of it, out of the bulging side pocket of his short trousers, and drew it backwards and forwards, and bobbed it up and down just in front of Cincinnatus' nose. But Cincinnatus would not play.

Cincinnatus sat up very stiff and straight, with

all his four paws in a row and his tail curled very tight over them, blinking his yellow eyes at the fire. For Cincinnatus was offended! Even cats have feelings. And on thinking it over, he came to the conclusion that he had not been treated with sufficient respect.

'Soup-pots and wooden spoons—fiddledeedee,' he said to himself in the cat-language. 'Why pervert a child's mind with such inane fictions?'

For you see Cincinnatus was not a common cat; being first cousin once removed, indeed, to the Sacristan's cat at Nullepart—who knew all the feast and fast days in the church calendar as well as the Sacristan himself, and had not eaten a mouse on a Friday for I cannot say how long. When you have a scholar in the family it obliges you to be dignified.

And so poor little Peter, as nothing and nobody would help to amuse him and pass away the time, pressed his two fat, little hands together in a sort of despair, and gave a terrible sigh.

'Bless the child, what possesses him?' cried Eliza again. 'Ah, my heart! How you made me jump!'

'What is the matter, Peter?' asked his mother.

'Oh! I don't believe Antony will ever come home,' said the boy, while the great tears began to run down over his chubby cheeks. 'And I am so tired of waiting. And I want so badly to know whether they have dressed the stable in the big church at Nullepart; and whether we shall really go there on Sunday, to see the dear baby Jesus, and the blessed Virgin, and good St. Joseph, and the donkeys and cows, you told me about. I have never seen them yet. And I want so dreadfully to go.'

Then his mother took up Peter in her arms, and sat down in the wooden chair in the chimney-corner, and held him gently on her lap.

'There, there,' she said, as she stroked his pretty hair, 'what cause have you to fret? The stable will be dressed all in good time; and the donkeys and cows certainly won't run away before Sunday. And St. Joseph and the blessed Virgin will be glad that a little lad like you should come and burn a candle before them—never fear. If the day is fair we will certainly all go to church on Sunday. What is to be will be, and Antony's coming late or early can make no difference. Patience is a great virtue, dear, little one—you cannot learn that too soon.'

But Cincinnatus sat up very stiff, though he was growing slightly sleepy; and still winked his yellow eyes at the fire. He was not at all sure that it was not incumbent upon him to spit at the charcoal-burner next time he saw him. It was an extreme measure certainly, and before adopting it he would have been glad to take his cousin the Sacristan's cat's opinion on the matter. Social position brings its responsibilities. Yet all the same, it is a fine thing to have a scholar in the family.

CHAPTER II.

WHICH INTRODUCES THE READER TO AN ADMIRER OF THE ANCIENT ROMANS.

NOW, Peter's father was a person of some consequence, or, to speak quite correctly, thought himself of some consequence, which, as you will probably find when you grow older, often comes to much the same thing. He had his own piece of land, and his own herd of cows, which the boys, in the spring time, would help Gustavus to drive, along with the cows of their neighbours, to the wide, grass lands that border the forest on the west, where the blue salvias, and gentians, and campanulas, and St. Bruno's white lilies grow in the long grass. But years ago Peter's father had been a soldier in the French army, and had fought in great battles, and had been in Italy, and even across the sea to Africa. He could tell surprising stories of sandy deserts, and camels, and lions, and Arabs, and a number of other remarkable things that he had seen during his travels. And when he went down, as he frequently did, and sat in the wine shop at Nullepart, everybody treated him with deference and distinction, and called him not plain Lepage, but Master Lepage, and listened respectfully to all that he had to say.

Then Master Lepage was very well pleased, and he would take his pipe out of his mouth, and spread out his hands like some celebrated orator, and give the company the benefit of his views upon any subject—even those he did not very well understand. For the great thing is to talk, if you want to make an impression upon society—the sense of that which you say is quite a secondary consideration. Lepage was a handsome man ; with a bright, grey eye, and a nose like a hawk's beak ; and a fine, grey moustache, the ends of which curled up till they nearly touched his eyebrows. He held himself very erect, so that even in his blue blouse and peg-top trousers, with a great, brown umbrella under his arm, he still looked every inch a soldier.

But Master Lepage, notwithstanding his superior knowledge of the world, did not always contrive to please his friends and companions. For he was—so he said—a philosophic politician; and, like most other philosophers and politicians, he sometimes became both tedious and irritable. On such occasions his voice would grow loud, and he would thump the table with his fist till the plates danced and the glasses rattled again; and the more the person with whom he was conversing smiled and apologised, while he differed from him in opinion, the louder his voice would grow, and the more he would thump the table, and stamp and violently declare that all who did not agree with him were idiots and dolts, and traitors.

He had two fixed ideas. He venerated the republican form of government, and he despised the Prussians. If one of his sons was idle, loitering over his work or complaining that he had too much to do, Master Lepage would say to him sternly:—
'Sluggard, you are unworthy to be the child of a glorious republic.'

Or if one of the cows kicked, when Gustavus was milking her, he would cry out:—'Hey then, thou blue imbecile, recollect that thou art the cow of a free citizen, and do not behave like a cut-throat Prussian!'

And during the long evenings of all the winters that little Peter could remember—they were not so very many, though, after all—when the supper was cleared away and the hearth swept, his father, after putting on a big pair of gold-rimmed spectacles, and drawing his chair close up to the table so that the lamp-light might fall full on his book, would read to himself the history of the famous Roman Republic. And always once or twice, during the course of the evening, he would lay down the book and take off his spectacles, and as he rubbed the glasses of them with his red pocket-handkerchief, would sigh to himself and say quite gently:—'Ah! but those were times worth living in! They had men worth looking at in those days.'

The elder of little Peter's brothers was named Antony. He was a smart, brisk young fellow. He was always in a little bit of a hurry and full of business. He liked to go down to the town to market. He liked to drive a sharp bargain, and when he had nothing else to do he would roam away to the railway station, and hang over the blue wooden railings at the back of the platform, staring at the crowded passenger or heavily laden freight trains going through to Paris, or over the frontier into Switzerland. And if he ever happened to catch sight of any soldiers on the trains, his eyes grew bright and his face eager, and he would whistle a stirring march as he walked home through the forest, and would chatter all the evening about the glorious fun he meant to have when the time came for him to serve his term in the army. And, at that, Master Lepage would look up from the pages of his Roman history book, and nod confidentially to his wife, and say:—

'Eh! our Antony is a fine fellow. He will help some day to thrash those rascally Prussians.'

But she would answer rather sadly:—

'That will be as the Lord pleases. There is sorrow and sin enough in the world already, it seems to me, without war to make it greater.'

Then Lepage would shrug his shoulders with an air of slight disgust, and say:—

'My wife, you are no doubt an excellent

woman. But your mind is narrow. Only a secular education, and, above all, a careful study of ancient history, can enable us to speak intelligently on these great questions.'

Then he would wipe his spectacles and return once again to the campaigns of the Romans.

Paul, the second boy, was very different to his brother. He was tall and lanky, with quiet, brown

eyes and straight, black hair. He had a great turn for mechanics, and made little Peter all manner of charming toys—mill-wheels that turned all splashing and sparkling in the clear water of the stream; or windmills, to set up in the garden, and scare the birds away from the fruit with their clatter, and many other pretty ingenious things. Paul did not talk much about himself; he was a quiet, silent fellow, but he was always busy with his fingers making little models of all the machinery he could see or get pictures of, and, though his father was not quite so partial to him as to Antony, he would sometimes say :—

'Eh! our Paul, too, will distinguish himself, and bring credit upon his family and country.'

Now on the particular evening that I was telling you about in the last chapter, Antony did not come in till quite late. The rest of the family had had their supper, and Eliza was grumbling to Gustavus as she rummaged about in the back kitchen.

'Why can't people be punctual?' she said. 'It would vex a saint to be kept muddling about till just upon bed-time unable to complete the day's work and wash up the plates and dishes. Those who come in late should go to bed supperless if I had my way.'

'Umph,' said Gustavus—which was a remarkably safe answer, since it meant chiefly nothing at all.

Master Lepage sat studying the story of the gallant Horatius, how he and two others defended the falling bridge over the river Tiber against all the host of Clusium and the allied cities. Paul, with a pocket-knife and a number of bits of wood on the table before him, was making a model of a force-pump. And Susan Lepage sat in the chimney corner knitting, little Peter on a stool at her feet resting his head against her knees. He was getting so sleepy that his eyes would shut though he tried very hard to keep them open. Sometimes his poor, little head nodded over all on one side; and then he woke up with a great start, dreaming that he had tumbled out of the old pear-tree in the garden, bump, on to the ground. And the dream was so vivid that it took him quite a minute and a half to remember where he was, and to realise that he was sitting on his own little stool in the kitchen, instead of lying on the asparagus bed under the pear-tree. But sleepy or not, Peter was determined not to go to bed till he had heard the news from Nullepart.

The longest waiting must needs end at last.

There was a sound of brisk footsteps, the door was thrown open, and Antony entered the kitchen, with the rush and bustle of a healthy, young whirlwind.

Peter was wide awake in a moment. He jumped up and caught hold of the skirt of his brother's blouse.

'Oh, tell me, tell me,' he cried, 'have they dressed the stable in the church, and can I go on Sunday and see it?'

Now, it is always a great mistake to rush at people with questions when they are full of their own affairs; and so little Peter found in this case. For Antony had some money to pay over to his father, and a great many things to say on his own account; and then, too, he was very hungry and wanted his supper, so he pushed poor Peter aside rather roughly, and told him to get out of the way and mind his own business, and intimated generally that he was an inconvenient and superfluous person.

Peter retired to his stool again feeling very

small. Between sleepiness and disappointment he was very much inclined to cry. Perhaps, indeed, he would have done so, had not Cincinnatus got up and rubbed gently against his legs, with a high back and a very upstanding tail, purring very loud, too, and saying as plain as cat-language could say it :—

'Console yourself. I, Cincinnatus, regret what has occurred. I am your friend. Confide in me. All will yet go well.'

For Cincinnatus was a cat of feeling, and never lost an opportunity of making himself agreeable if he could do it without loss of dignity. However, when Antony had transacted his business, and eaten his supper, and bragged a little about his own performances of one sort and another, he became a trifle ashamed of having behaved so roughly to his little brother. He did not say so, for few people have courage to make a public confession of their faults. But he described, with great animation, how the workmen and the good sisters were busy in the church ; how bright everybody said the Virgin's blue mantle would be, how there was real straw in the stable, how charmingly natural the cattle and the donkey looked, and how ingeniously a lamp would be arranged—just like the star, in fact—to shine above the manger. Peter felt satisfied again. But he was still a little hurt; so he sat quiet and rubbed Cincinnatus' head in silence, though there were a hundred and one questions he was longing to ask.

'You will come with us, *mon ami*?' said Susan Lepage, looking across at her husband, who had just laid down his book, and was wiping his spectacles with his red handkerchief.

'Your sons will take good care of you,' he answered. 'As for me, I will keep house.'

'It is the first time we take our little Peter,' she said, and there was a pleading tone in her voice.

The little boy loved both his father and mother; though perhaps he loved his mother best, for he was rather afraid of his father sometimes. But now for some reason he grew very bold. He jumped up and trotted across the kitchen, and climbed up on his father's knee.

'Oh, it will be so beautiful,' he said—'And we

shall all be so happy—do come, father, do come too.'

Master Lepage looked at him very kindly out of his shrewd, grey eyes, and gently pinched his cheek.

'No, no, my son,' he answered, 'go with your mother and your brothers. These shows are admirable for pious women and for the young. But you see I am no longer very young, and they no longer greatly interest me. Those who think deeply upon politics and philosophy outgrow the satisfaction that others derive from such devout illusions. Every age has its appropriate pastimes. Go, my children. As for me, I will remain at home, read the newspaper, and pursue my studies in ancient history.'

'Cannot you think of something better than the doings of those unhappy, old heathens for one day in the week, *mon ami*?' asked his wife.

Little Peter looked up at her quickly. She had laid aside her knitting, and coming across the room placed her hand lightly on her husband's shoulder.

Master Lepage made a grimace, moved a little in his chair, and smiled good-humouredly at her.

'Ah! my dear, you are the best of women,' he said.

'Then why will you not oblige me?'

Lepage pressed his lips together and put up his eyebrows.

'There are points,' he said, 'on which compliance would be a mere manifestation of weakness. We will not discuss the situation. About those small matters upon which we do not, unfortunately, quite agree, it is wise to maintain silence. There are your three sons—an escort worthy of a Roman matron! Be contented, then. I remain at home.'

Susan Lepage turned away, and calling to Eliza bade her clear the table.

'Indeed, is it worth while? It will be breakfast time directly,' replied Eliza, who was still in a bad temper at Antony having been late for supper.

Susan Lepage looked up at the cuckoo clock in the corner.

'It is late,' she said. 'Come, come, Peter, we will go upstairs; it is long past your bedtime.'

But the boy did not want to go to bed. He felt a little disturbed and unhappy, and wanted Lepage more than ever to go with the rest of the family on Sunday to church at Nullepart. So he rubbed his black head against his father's shoulder coaxingly:—

'Mother wants you to go, and we all want it. Do please go with us to the church on Sunday.'

Master Lepage took the child and stood him down on the floor in front of him.

'Go to bed, when you are told to,' he said. 'Obedience was a virtue greatly prized by those grand old Romans.'

'Out of the mouth of babes—' murmured Susan Lepage, gently.

For some reason this observation appeared to incense her husband.

'Ten thousand plagues!' he burst out vehemently. 'Twenty thousand cut-throat Prussians! This is a conspiracy. Can I not stay at home when I please? Can I not sit peaceably in my own kitchen, without cabals and flagrant acts of insubordination? The rights of a husband and father are supreme and without limit, I tell you—read the domestic history of the ancient Romans.'

Susan Lepage waited till her husband had finished speaking; and then taking poor, frightened, little Peter by the hand, she said calmly :—

'Do not trouble your father any more, my child. He has his reasons for remaining at home, and doubtless they are good ones.'

Perhaps it was a dream—for Peter was very tired

'GO TO BED WHEN YOU ARE TOLD.'

Page 34.

and sleepy, and it came to him when he was snugly tucked up in his little bed, just before his mother put out the candle and left him alone with a faint glimmer of starlight coming in at the uncurtained window at the end of the room. Perhaps it was a dream; but certainly he seemed to hear Master Lepage's voice saying softly:—

'Forgive me, my wife. I was over hasty. Your path appears to lie in one direction and mine in another, at present; but let us both be tolerant. Who knows but that they may yet meet in the end!'

Then someone stooped down over the little boy's bed and kissed him. Yes, it must have been his father, for on his forehead he felt the rough scrape of a thick moustache.

CHAPTER III.

WHICH IMPROVES OUR ACQUAINTANCE WITH THE GRASS-HOPPER MAN.

'I AM going to Nullepart on Sunday,' cried little Peter.

'*Pfui*! what a traveller,' answered the charcoal-burner. 'And how do you go? In a coach and four, on the back of a fiery dragon, in the giant's seven-league boots, or flying through the air with the wild ducks, there, crying "Quack, quack, quack, we are all going south because the snow is coming?"'

'I shall walk, of course, like a big boy,' said little Peter. 'But the snow isn't coming just yet, is it?'

'They all say it will be here in a day or two.'

John Paqualin shook his head, and looked up at the sky. He was sitting on the rough, wooden bench set against the southern wall of his hut, with his back bent, and his elbows resting on his thin knees. Little Peter climbed up on to the bench beside him. It was rather difficult, you see, because the bench was a very high one, to suit the length of the charcoal-burner's long legs.

'Who are they?' asked the boy, as soon as he had settled himself comfortably. He tried to lean forward with his elbows on his knees like his companion; but his short legs were dangling, and his feet were far off the ground, and he did not find it altogether easy to keep his balance.

'Who are they?' he asked.

'Oh, the earth spirits, who live underground, and the air spirits, who wander up and down the sky. Look at the great arc of white light they are setting up in the north-east as a signal. And the wild ducks, flying overhead. And the moaning in the pine-trees. And Madelon, the old sow there; see how she runs about with her mouth full of grass, wanting to make herself a lair, because she sees the storm-wind coming. They are all telling what will happen. They are wiser than men. They know beforehand. Men only know afterwards.'

Paqualin paused a moment, and sat staring at Madelon, the old black sow, with her floppety ears, as she ran to and fro, and grouted about in the heaps of charcoal refuse and in the tumble-down garden fence—half smothered in tall withered grass and weeds—grunting and barking the while like one distracted.

'Everything in the world talks to me,' he continued, speaking slowly. 'All day long, all night long, the air is full of voices.'

Peter wriggled himself a little further back on the bench, for, in the excitement of conversation, he had slipped very near the edge of it and was in great danger of falling head first on to the ground.

'I don't hear them,' he said presently.

Paqualin laughed. His laugh was cracked and shrill, like his voice; and Peter was always a trifle startled by it somehow.

'Never hear them, little Peter,' he cried, 'never hear them. A few men will call you a poet, but most men will only call you mad, if you do.'

'What is mad?' asked Peter. He felt very much interested. 'Is it a good or a bad thing?'

The charcoal-burner looked round at the boy sharply, with his mouth a little open. His strange eyes were glowing dull red. He waited a minute before replying.

'Eh,' he said, 'what an innocent! Why, it is a good thing, of course. An excellent, splendid, glorious thing. Look at me, little Peter. I'll tell you a secret. Can you keep it? Here—quite close—I'll whisper—I am mad—yes, that's the secret. A grand one. See all the blessings it brings me. I live alone in the wood and burn charcoal.'

'Yes,' said Peter, 'I should like that.'

'I have no wife or child to bother me. On feast-days, when I was a lad, the pretty girls never plagued me to dance with them, or asked me to steal kisses.' The charcoal-burner laughed again

—' I am saved from all sins of pride and vanity. Think what a gain!—for as I go down the street, the very children tell me my faults, crying, "Look at the grasshopper legs, look at the crook-back;" and the women shut their eyes and turn their heads away, saying, "Heaven avert the bad omen! What a frightful fellow!" Such observations, little Peter, are sharp discipline; and teach humility more thoroughly than any penance the priest can lay on you. Oh, yes! no doubt it is a capital thing to be mad. It saves you a deal of trouble—nobody cares for you, nurses you when you're sick, feeds you when you're hungry, mourns for you when you die.'

Paqualin laughed again, and getting up stretched his long, ungainly limbs, and shook himself till his hair hung like a red cloud about his stooping shoulders.

'Ah! ha, it's splendid,' he cried, 'all alone with the spirits and voices, with the beasts, and the trees, and the rain, and the starlight. No one to love you but the fire when you feed it with branches, or the swine when you drive them back to their stye in the twilight.'

Now, to tell the truth, poor little Peter was becoming rather confused and nervous, with all this wild, incomprehensible talk of the charcoal-burner's. He had never seen his friend in this strange humour before. And he felt as much alarmed and embarrassed as he would have done if that well-conducted animal Cincinnatus had suddenly turned upon him, with bristling hair and a great tail, spitting and swearing, in the middle of their innocent games of play. He sat very still, staring anxiously at his companion.

But when Paqualin threw himself down on the bench again, and putting his lean, brown face very close to little Peter's, said to him with a sort of cry:—

'Think of it, think of it, child, nobody, day nor night, all through the long years of life, nobody ever to love you!'—the boy's embarrassment changed into absolute fear, and he scrambled down off the bench in a great hurry, hardly able to keep from sobbing.

'If you please, John Paqualin, I should like to go home to my mother,' he said; and then he trotted away as fast as he could along the black cinder-path across the little garden.

'Mother, mother,' echoed the charcoal-burner. 'Sweet, fair wife, and sweet mother! Have pity, dear Lord, on those who may have neither.'

Then he got up, and walked after the child, in his awkward way, calling gently to him:—

'Here, little mouse, come here. Don't run away so fast. There is nothing to hurt you.'

Peter had nearly reached the garden gate; but there in the opening stood Madelon, the sow, grunting and snorting, her great jaws working, and her wicked, little eyes twinkling.

'Come, come,' called Paqualin again, coaxingly. 'There are no more disquieting secrets to tell you. Never fear. See now, I have a box of nuts indoors, under my bed—beauties—beauties; will you try them? Cr-r-rack go the shells, out pop the nice kernels—crunch, crunch, crunch, between sharp, white, little teeth eating them all up. Eh! nuts are appetising, are they? You will not run away just yet, then, will you, dear little mouse.'

Now Peter would have felt a great deal safer at home it is true; but in the first place, there stood the hideous Madelon blocking the way, and he was very much afraid of her. And then in the second place, he did not wish to be uncivil to his old friend the charcoal-burner. So, finally, he went back, and climbed up the high bench again.

'I will not have any of those nuts, though, please,' he said decidedly. For he wished Paqualin to understand that it was not greediness but friendship that made him return.

'No nuts!' cried the charcoal-burner, smiling kindly at him. 'Eh, what a proud, little soul.'

And then John Paqualin really became delightful. And as he and the little boy sat together in the shelter of the high pine-trees, and of the brown, wooden wall of the tumble-down dwelling-house behind them, he told many most interesting stories. For, you see, the charcoal-burner, perhaps from living so much alone, perhaps from being what some persons call 'mad,' knew a number of things which you could not find in the pages of the very largest Encyclopædia of Universal Information — though they really are every bit as true as half the information you would find there. He knew all about the elves who live in the fox-glove bells; and the water-nixies who haunt the stream side; and about the gnomes who work with tiny spades and pickaxes, searching for the precious metals underground. And he could tell where the will-of-the-wisp gets the light for his lantern, with which he dances over bogs and marshy places, trying to lead weak-minded and unscientific travellers astray; and he knew all about the pot of fairy gold that stands just where the base of the rainbow touches the earth, and which moves away and away as you run to find it, shifting its ground forever, so that those who will seek it in the end come home hot, and breathless, and angry, and empty handed, for all their pains. And he could also tell of the old black dwarf who lives in a cave in the heart of the forest, which no one can ever find, though they may search for it for a year and a day; and who, being a mischievous and ill-conditioned dwarf, bewitches the cows so that they go dry; and the hens so that they steal their nests and lay their eggs in all manner of holes and corners, instead of in the hen-roosts like right-minded, well-conducted fowls; and who rides the horses all night long in the stable, so that when the carter goes in, in the dewy morning, to give them their fodder, he finds them trembling and starting and bathed in sweat; and who turns the cream sour in summer, or sits on the handle of the churn—though you can't see him—so that though the good housewife turns and turns, till her arms and back ache, and the heat stands in drops on her forehead, the butter will not come and the day's work is well-nigh wasted.

And Paqualin could tell the story, moreover, of the dirty little boy, Eli, who insisted on eating raw turnips and cabbages, and distressing his friends and relatives by picking bits out of the pig pail, instead of sitting up to table like a little gentleman, and who utterly refused to have his hair combed or his face washed :—

'And, at last, one night,' said the charcoal-burner, 'as a punishment for all his nasty ways, the fairies came and turned him into a great black crow, which flew out of the bedroom window in the chilly dawn. You may often hear him now, little Peter, croaking in the tree-tops, or see him skulking about the farmyard and gardens looking out for scraps and refuse.'

'How long ago was he turned into a crow?' asked Peter.

'Eh, many and many a year ago,' answered the charcoal-burner. 'I saw him only yesterday, and he has grown quite old and grey. But the time of his probation will not be over yet awhile, for bad habits are slow to die, though quick enough to breed in us, little Peter. I throw him a crust of bread now and again, the poor old villain. I've a sort of fellow feeling for him, you see, for I am an ugly, old vagabond too.'

'Bless the child, there he is at last! Ah,

my poor heart, how it beats with all this running.'

The speaker was Eliza. She stood on the other side of the tumble-down, garden fence, with her hand pressed to her side, and a shawl over her head. She was breathing very hard. Eliza was one of those persons who like to make the most of an injury.

'Come home, Peter, come at once,' she went on. 'Don't you know it's half an hour past dinner-time? Here have I been trapesing half over the country to find you—a pretty occupation for a respectable, young, servant woman like me, too. All the men were out, and nothing would do but that I must go racing about like a wild creature, wasting good shoe leather in looking for you. Ah! my poor heart.'

Eliza leant up against the fence and panted a little.

As Peter got down off the bench, Paqualin bent forward and patted the boy's curly head.

'Run away, little mouse,' he said, 'but come again some day and see me.'

'Am I to wait here all night,' cried Eliza,

'for you, Peter? Have you not had enough yet of the society of his highness the charcoal-burner? No, no, don't speak to me,' she added, addressing

Paqualin. 'I have no desire to hold any communication with you. Why, merely seeing you as you pass makes me squint for an hour afterwards. Come along, child.'

And seizing Peter's fat, pudgy hand in her large, red one, Eliza marched him off at a sharp pace down the forest path.

'Hey ho, hey ho, life is a bit long for some of us,' said the charcoal-burner.

CHAPTER IV.

WHICH LEAVES SOME AT HOME AND TAKES SOME TO CHURCH.

LITTLE Peter woke up very early on Sunday morning, feeling excited and glad. He sat up on end in bed, but he had to rub his eyes very hard and get the sleep out of them before he could remember exactly what there was to be so very glad about. When he did remember, he was so much delighted that he was compelled to express his feelings in some rather violent manner. He went on all fours and burrowed very quick, like a rabbit, head first, down under the clothes to the bottom of the bed, and then rushed up again, with very red cheeks, puffing, and pushing his curly hair out of his eyes. But it really was not light yet

—only the rushlight his mother burnt at night glimmered feebly in the corner. Peter could hear Master Lepage snoring peacefully in his bed on the other side of the wooden partition which divided the big room into two unequal halves—the small half for little Peter and his little bed, and the large half for his father and mother and their large bed. It would be a long while yet before his mother got up and called him to her to help dress and wash him, for Gustavus, the cowherd, had only just gone downstairs from his attic, clumpety-clump with his big, heavy boots over the stairs, and he always got up long before anybody else.

Peter wondered what he could do to amuse himself till it was time to dress. And then it struck him as just possible that when Gustavus went down into the kitchen he might have left the door open, and that in that case Cincinnatus, the cat, might have stepped upstairs and be waiting outside on the landing—it had happened so once before on a very delightful and never to be forgotten occasion. Peter waited a moment and held his breath listening, for it seemed to him extremely adventurous to be on the move so very early in the morning. He was not quite sure whether the little, hairy house-bogies and hobgoblins who undoubtedly, so Eliza said at least, wander about the empty rooms and chase each other up and down the silent passages and stairways every night, with impish frolic and laughter, when we are all safe in bed, might not still be holding their revels ; and he knew, at least Eliza said so, that it was extremely unlucky for any person to see them, for they don't like to be looked at by mortal eyes, and will come and sit on your pillow, and tickle your nose with a feather out of the bedding, and squat on your chest, till you feel as though you lay under the weight of a mountain, and treat you in a number of other odious and disturbing ways. It made the cold shivers run down Peter's back as he sat up there, in his little, white night-shirt, even to think of coming face to face with the hairy goblins and bogies.

But then, on the other hand, the society of Cincinnatus would be so very delightful. Peter slipped one sturdy, bare leg down over the side of the bed. Ah! how cold the smooth boards of the floor felt! However, the other leg very soon followed. Then he crept across the room very quietly, avoiding the oak chest, and the chairs, and the corner of the high cupboard, with his mother's initials and the date of her wedding-day carved on the doors of it; and, when he reached the door, paused, listening at the keyhole. Oh, dear me, there really was something outside on the landing moving about stealthily on small, soft feet. Little Peter's heart stood still. Was it dear, old Cincinnatus, or a dreadful, roundabout, hairy hobgoblin?

At last he plucked up courage to put his lips close to the keyhole, and whisper in a rather trembling voice :—

'Pussy, puss, Cincinnatus, oh, please, is that you?'

'Miau,' answered Cincinnatus, quite composedly and comfortably.

In a great hurry little Peter opened a crack of the door.

'Oh! come in quick, please, Cincinnatus,' he said.

But cats of quality never permit themselves to be hurried. Cincinnatus came just half-way through the door, then he stopped and rubbed himself—very tall—up against the side-post and purred; and then, stretching out his fore legs as far as ever he could, sharpened his claws, crick, crack, crick, crack, on the boards of the bedroom flooring.

'Oh! do be quick, Cincinnatus,' said the little boy under his breath again; and to hasten matters, he gave the cat a poke in the ribs with his cold bare toes.

'Miau,' cried Cincinnatus quite sharply, jumping on one side, for he was taken rather by surprise. Subsequently he added in the cat language:—
'Manners, my good child, manners! Let us before all things cultivate a polite address and a calm, unagitated exterior.'

Meanwhile Peter had succeeded in shutting the door quietly, and that, to his great relief, without catching a single glimpse of one of the blobbetybodied, spindle-legged house-bogies. He pattered across the room as fast as ever he could, and jumped into his warm bed again.

'He is young and inexperienced,' murmured

"Oh! come in quick, please, Cincinnatus."

Cincinnatus reflectively. 'I am magnanimous. I scorn to bear malice.'

And he, too, jumped into the warm bed.

Now, this was really charming. Little Peter pushed up the bedclothes in front, making them into a snug, little, dark cavern, inside which there was just room enough for himself and Cincinnatus.

'See,' he said, 'we will play at robbers. I will be the captain and you shall be my first lieutenant.'

But unfortunately, Cincinnatus did not seem to care very much about that particular game. He had arrived at an age and temper of mind at which material comfort is far more valuable than pleasures derived from a lively exercise of the imagination. Perhaps you do not quite understand what that means? Well, so much the better. For my part, I hope you never may understand it. There are a number of things in this world that it is very much the best to be ignorant about if you can possibly manage it. Cincinnatus, anyway, understood it well enough, so he tucked his fore legs under his chest, until nothing was visible of them but just the furry elbows, and laid his tail neatly along his soft side, and settled himself down on the warm sheet, with his eyes more than half shut, purring all the while as loud as if he had got a small steam-engine inside him.

'That's not the way to play at robbers,' said little Peter.

But Cincinnatus only purred a trifle louder. It was rather provoking. Still, Peter was too glad of the cat's comfortable company, and was, moreover, really too sweet-tempered a boy to get cross and angry. So he just lay down on his stomach, resting his chin in one hand, while with the other he gently rubbed Cincinnatus about the ears; and amused himself by thinking of the nice, new clothes that lay folded up on the chair at the bottom of his bed, and of the representation of the stable, and the manger in which the Infant Saviour was cradled, that he hoped to see in the great church in the town, before the day was done. And meanwhile, the pale dawn broadened over the dark stretches of the great pine forest, and the cows lowed as Gustavus drove them out to pasture, and Eliza bustled down stairs to begin dusting and sweeping, and making ready the savoury Sunday breakfast.

And at last his mother, with her sweet, pale face, got up and washed and dressed him, listening as tenderly, as only mothers know how, to his happy, prattle, and his simple morning prayer.

'Ask the dear Lord to send a special blessing to us all to-day,' she said.

'May I ask Him to send a blessing to my friend John Paqualin, too?' asked Peter. 'He told me yesterday he should never have anybody to love him, and that it saved him a great deal of trouble. But he doesn't look as if it made him happy, does he, mother?'

'Alas, no, poor soul,' said Susan Lepage. 'Yes, pray for him, also, little one, pray that the long disgrace and lonely sorrow of his life here may be counted unto him for righteousness hereafter, and I will say Amen.'

It must have been quite half-past eight o'clock before they were all ready to start for Nullepart. Eliza was going too, you see, and she was furiously busy up to the very last moment. Consequently she was rather late, and rushed out of the house after the rest of the party, pinning her blue shawl, and giving sundry pats to the crown of her stiff, white, muslin cap, to make sure it sat quite straight over her plaits of hair behind.

'Eh, but you are smart, Eliza,' said Gustavus, opening his eyes very wide, as he rested the two pails of water he was carrying on the ground for a moment, and rubbed his elbows, which ached a little with the weight.

'*Imbécile!* do not detain me!' cried Eliza, haughtily—though, in truth, she was prodigiously gratified by the cowherd's observation. ' Don't you see how breathless and flurried I am with all the work? Bless me, where's my prayer-book? Oh! thank you, yes, Gustavus, tied up in my pocket-handkerchief. Of course—I knew where it was— at least, I should have found out for myself directly. Good-bye, Gustavus, take care of yourself; and remember the evening's milk is to be set on the left-hand shelf, two from the bottom.'

Eliza pursed up her mouth and nodded, as she walked away with a very impressive swinging of petticoats.

' Poor young man, his head is completely turned,'

she said to herself. 'But then, what wonder? My appearance in my *fête* day clothes has always been a subject of remark and respectful admiration!'

'Farewell, my wife; enjoy to the full the emotions called forth by the pious exhibition you are about to witness. They are becoming to your sex. Boys, take good care of your mother; and conduct yourselves in all things as worthy sons of our glorious Republic.'

Master Lepage raised his soft felt hat from his head, as he spoke, with an elegant flourish; but whether in compliment to his wife or in honour of the democratic form of government, I really cannot say.

At that moment the charcoal-burner came hurriedly from the narrow forest path, that led from his hut, on to the open space outside the farmhouse. Madelon, the sow, ran beside him, shaking her lean sides as she ran, and grunting now and then, apparently with pleasure at being taken out walking. Sometimes she bundled up against her master's long, thin legs, nearly knocking him over; sometimes she stopped and forced her ugly snout into a tuft of grass or weeds by the wayside. The charcoal-burner's red hair streamed out behind him as he came rapidly along; his strange eyes were dull and vacant as those of a sleep-walker.

'I have a message,' he cried hoarsely—'a message to you from the beasts, and the birds, from the pine-trees, and the storm-clouds and the voices. All night long they have told it me, over and over again.'

Paqualin, a wild, ragged, unkempt figure, came up close to Master Lepage, who stood there erect and superior as a general officer on parade, surrounded with his family and servants—Gustavus had left his pails of water and joined the little company—in their Sunday best, and all animated with pleasant expectation of a holiday, in which amusement promised to be agreeably mingled with spiritual edification.

'Well, well, out with it quickly then, my good fellow, this wonderful message of yours,' Lepage said, in a bantering, patronising tone. 'You see my wife and my sons here are just ready to start on a long walk. I cannot have them delayed.'

'They must not go, or you must go with them,' cried the charcoal-burner. He stretched out his hands like a man in the dark groping for something he cannot find. 'My head is troubled,' he went on. 'I cannot tell you plainly; but I have an aching in all my bones which foretells misfortune. And I say, they must not go.'

'Pooh,' said Lepage. 'Your head is troubled, just so. But when people's heads are troubled they had best keep at home and not trouble their neighbours into the bargain with all their crazy fancies. Calm yourself, Paqualin. And as for you,' added Lepage, nodding encouragingly to his wife and the boys, 'forward, march. Do not let this untoward little incident affect the pleasures of the day.'

But Susan Lepage looked kindly and compassionately at the charcoal-burner, and then turning to her husband, said :—

'Have a moment's patience with him, *mon ami*; let us at least hear what he has to say.'

'Yes, give me time,' cried Paqualin imploringly. 'There are so many of you staring at me.—Ah! I begin to remember. You must go with them if they go, for the snow is coming, Master Lepage. The storm hung out its streaming, white flag in the northeast yesterday, and the wild ducks flew south; there were signs in the earth and in the heavens, and in my ears the sound of many voices. Do not let your wife and children go. The snow will be here before evening, and the way will be difficult to find, and the house door will stand open long into the night before the feet of those you love cross the threshold.'

The charcoal-burner spoke as though he was so certain of the truth of that which he said, and his voice sounded so sad, that poor little Peter felt quite dismayed. Even Eliza had no opprobrious observation to make, and as for Gustavus, he stood with his big mouth wide open, staring as if he saw a ghost.

Master Lepage, however, remained quite unmoved; and his composure was very reassuring.

'Well, well, my good fellow,' he said, 'I for

one need no further proof that your head is very much troubled, so much so indeed that if I had my way you should find a lodging for a time in the *Maison Dieu* at Nullepart—an excellent institution, which is calculated to cure troubled heads, or at all events to restrain the possessors of them from being inconvenient to other people. But the worst of it is,' Lepage added, rather angrily, 'that this superstitious nonsense is infectious. You, for instance, my wife, begin to look quite disconcerted.'

Lepage folded his arms, and nodded his head argumentatively, quite as though he had been addressing an audience in the wine shop.

'Now I put it to you,' he said, 'the day is mild and even sunshiny at present. And which, pray, is likely to be the best weather prophet? I, Francis Louis Lepage, householder, citizen, veteran, and I may add philosophic-politician and student of ancient history, or that poor half-wit—unsound, as anyone can see, both in mind and body?'

'Of course the grasshopper's afraid of the snow,' chimed in Antony, switching at Madelon, the sow, with the little stick he held in his hand. 'It puts his fiddle out of tune.'

Then Antony laughed rather loud, as people do sometimes when they have made a joke they are not sure is a very good one.

'For shame, Antony,' said his mother quickly. And John Paqualin turned on the lad, his eyes glowing like live coals.

'Ah! it is noble and generous in a handsome fellow like you to taunt me and scoff at me! Heaven pay you back in your own coin.'

Eliza gave a scream, and seized Gustavus by the arm as though she required protection from some most fearful danger.

'For the love of the saints, ma'am, let us go on, and get out of the way of this wild animal,' she said, in a very loud whisper. 'He looks wicked enough to commit a crime. Keep off, Gustavus! What are you thinking about, catching hold like that of a respectable, young, servant woman?'

'Why it was you who caught hold of me, Eliza,' answered the cowherd mildly.

F

Paqualin, meanwhile, looked round the little group with a sort of despair in his poor ugly face.

'It is all useless,' he said; 'you will not listen to or believe me. I only get jeered at. You all despise me.'

He turned away with a bitter cry, and shambled off into the forest.

'Good-bye, dear John Paqualin, good-bye.—No, I won't hush, Eliza. I love him, he is a very kind friend to me.—Good-bye, dear John Paqualin,' little Peter called after him.

He felt very very sorry for the poor charcoal-burner.

'Whoof,' went Madelon, the sow, making a run at Cincinnatus—who sat washing his face on the clean flags just outside the door of the farm-house—and taking him so by surprise that he leapt up, with a prodigious tail, on to the window ledge, without even waiting to scratch. Then she cantered off, grunting and shaking her great bristly, floppety ears, after her master.

'Next time I see the charcoal-burner, it will

'YOU ALL DESPISE ME.'

Page 66.

undoubtedly be my duty to spit at him,' said Cincinnatus to himself in the cat-language. 'After that which has just occurred, I feel it is quite unnecessary to take any second opinion upon the subject.'

'Forward, march,' cried Master Lepage gaily. 'Enjoy yourselves. Let no thought of that unfortunate being's prognostications disturb you. The day will be charming.'

And so, after all, they started for Nullepart.

CHAPTER V.

WHICH IS BOTH SOCIAL AND RELIGIOUS.

NOW, undoubtedly, it is extremely easy to most persons not to believe a thing if they do not wish to believe it. And very soon our friends, wending their way along the soft moist forest path, in the languid December sunshine, began to forget about John Paqualin and his alarming warning.

'It was all spite,' said Eliza, tossing her head, white muslin cap and all, with a great show of dignity. 'He hates me because I won't receive his advances and always keep him at a proper distance. It was just a trick to deprive a poor, hard-working, young woman of a well-earned holiday.'

'I think he was wrong about the weather,' remarked Paul quietly. 'It's generally colder before snow.'

'He ought to be shut up in the madhouse, as my father suggested,' said Antony, who was still smarting from the reproof his mother had given him. 'I'd have all those sort of fellows kept under lock and key. There ought to be a law about it. They've no right to be about loose.'

'You are young, my son,' said Susan Lepage, 'and the young, too often, are thoughtless and cruel. Perhaps life will teach you, among other lessons, to be merciful if you would obtain mercy.'

Antony's handsome face grew very sulky. 'You're always scolding me for something or other,' he said crossly.

Meanwhile our little Peter was very happy. He had been sorry for the charcoal-burner, it is true; but he would have been very much more sorry not to go to Nullepart. A light breeze ruffled the dark branches of the pine-trees; here and there a scarlet or yellow leaf still hung on the brambles that grew on the skirts of the wood; the little birds looked at him merrily with their round, bright eyes, as they flew chirping to and fro among the trees and bushes. As to the snow, Peter did not give it a

thought, as he ran, just like a little dog, first a long way on in front of the rest of the party, and then dawdled ever so far behind them—looking at the quaint little huts, and houses, and castles that the pine needles make where they fall and gather on the small twigs and branches at the base of the younger trees; and then, seeing that his mother and brothers had got on a long way ahead of him, scuttled up to them again in a great fuss and hurry, with very red cheeks, and a curious bumping at his heart, what with excitement and exercise, and just a trifle of fright, too, lest the old dwarf whom John Paqualin had told him about should suddenly nod and grin at him from under the pine boughs, saying:—

'Hey, my fine fellow, so we've met at last!' But I suppose the black dwarf was plotting mischief at home within the recesses of his mysterious cavern on that particular Sunday morning; for though he kept a very sharp look-out, little Peter saw no trace of his naughty, mocking face, even where the path was narrowest and the pine-trees thickest.

Now the town of Nullepart is an exceedingly ancient place, as you will gather from its name if you are anything of a scholar. It lies down in a remote valley along the banks of a river, with hills on either hand clothed below with oak, and beech, chestnut, and walnut, and, at their summits, crowned with pine-trees, that make a dark, ragged, saw-like edge against the sky. Some of the houses in the main street are built of stone, and roofed with fine, red, fluted tiles; but the major part of them are of wood, like the farm-house in the forest, with deep eaves, and quaint gables and stairways, and galleries. And I am sorry to say that the good people of Nullepart are somewhat old-fashioned in their habits, and do not pay quite as strict a regard to cleanliness as might be desired; and permit their ducks, and chickens, and pigs to walk about the crooked streets along with the foot-passengers, in rather too friendly and confidential a manner.

But little Peter, never having seen any other town, thought Nullepart a very fine place indeed; and quite believed that nowhere else in the world were there such grand houses, or such inviting shops, or so many people, or half so much chatter and bustle. You see the justice of our opinions is very much dependent upon the extent of our experience—a fact which few persons always manage to bear in mind, at least where their own opinions are concerned—

GOING TO CHURCH.

Page 72

with the opinions of their neighbours it is, of course, different.

Little Peter clung rather tight to his mother's hand on one side, and to his brother Paul's on the other, for he was somewhat afraid of being lost in the crowd and never found again. Antony did not offer to hold the little boy's hand. He walked on the other side of his mother, with his cap set jauntily over one ear and his handsome face all smiles again. He nodded and said good-day to all his acquaintances, and stared hard at all the pretty girls when he passed them, as a young man should who has a good opinion of himself and who intends some day to be a soldier.

But if little Peter thought Nullepart street dangerously full of people, what did he think when passing under the carved porch, and pushing aside the heavy, leathern curtain that hung across the doorway, he entered the church itself, still clinging tightly to his mother's hand ?

He could see nothing but trousers and petticoats, the broad backs of men, and the comfortable backs of women—it would be uncivil to call them broad, too, you know; you should select your adjectives carefully in speaking of ladies—and the straight backs of lads, and the slim, neat backs of young girls all around him; while the close, heavy air of the church was full of the hum of many voices, and the shuffling of many feet over the stone pavement.

'Ouf, how hot!' said Eliza, in a loud whisper, unpinning her blue shawl. 'Heaven forgive me, but it's like being in a saucepan with the lid on. Why, there's my cousin Ursula Jacqueline Lambert. Ah, my dear cousin! how have you been this long while? Yes, it is seldom we meet. And time passes and leaves its mark behind it. Not that I change much—no, the saints be praised, I keep my looks. But I see you have altered. Well, it cannot be helped. Your husband is a good, faithful soul, and I daresay he doesn't observe it. There's the advantage of having married an old man. His eyes grow dim just in time—now with me. . . .'

But Peter did not hear any more of Eliza's conversation, for his mother moved forward into the middle of the nave of the church, from whence it was possible to see the high altar, with its lights and flowers, and the great picture behind it, of which the people of Nullepart are very proud, for it was painted by a famous artist and is worth a great deal of money, and is, moreover, so dark with age, and, perhaps, with a proportion of dirt as well, that it affords an immense amount of interesting conversation, as nobody has ever yet discovered what subject it represents.

Priests in rich vestments stood before the altar, their backs looking like those of great gold and silver beetles; and there were boys with tall candles, and boys chanting; and the plaintive sound of the organ; and many persons kneeling on low chairs or on the rough pavement saying their prayers. Susan Lepage knelt down too; and little Peter stood bareheaded close beside her. The church, somehow, seemed very different to what he had expected. It was very large and high, and the painted windows up in the roof let in but scanty light. It seemed to

Peter a very mysterious place; and he felt a wee bit frightened.

At last Susan rose again from her knees.

'Now for thy pleasure, little one,' she said, looking lovingly at the child. 'Where is the stable, Antony?'

'It is there,' he answered, pointing to the southern aisle of the church. 'I've just been to see; but the crowd is so thick about it we must wait awhile—we can't get through yet.'

Susan Lepage sat down on one of the low, rush-bottomed chairs, and took Peter on her lap.

'All in good time,' she said. 'Antony will let us know when to be moving. Meanwhile, we will rest. Your poor, little legs must be tired.'

Presently a stout, genial-looking, old gentleman, in a black cassock and funny, little, black cape, came up to them. He wore a black skull-cap, too, for the church was draughty, and his head was bald, save just at the back, where his short, bristly, white hair stood out like a neat trimming round the edge of his cap.

'Well, well, Susan Lepage, it isn't often that we see you here, now,' he said. 'Don't move, don't move, my good woman. Ah, yes! I know the walk is long and fatiguing; you would come oftener if you could. The spirit is willing, as it is written, but the flesh is weak. Yet you do well to come to

day, and bring these fine lads, your sons, with you. The good God remembers those who remember Him. But where is the husband?'

Peter looked at his mother as the priest asked this question, and it seemed to him that for some reason she seemed troubled and sad.

'Ah, my father, he has remained at home to

keep house. We live, as you know, in a lonely place.'

The priest smiled and shook his head.

'Exactly,' he said, 'I understand. Politics have a word to say in the matter, though, haven't they?'

But Susan Lepage did not smile in return.

'Alas, my father!' she said.

Peter stared at both speakers wonderingly. He did not understand what they meant. But then it must be admitted there are a good many things we do not quite understand at five years old.

'Do not vex yourself,' answered the priest kindly. 'It is written that the faithful wife may save her husband. All times are in the hands of God. That which He has ordained cannot fail to be accomplished.'

Then he laid his hand gently on little Peter's round, black head, saying :—

'And this is your youngest, the autumn child, who brings the blessing to the house?'

'Yes,' she said. 'He has come for the first time to burn a candle before the Infant Jesus. But the worshippers are so many that as yet we have been unable to get a sight of the stable.'

Just then Eliza bustled up.

'Ah,' she exclaimed, 'one thing is certain, my poor cousin's temper is sadly soured with age. I made myself agreeable to her, in the assurance that she would at least ask me in to dinner.—Forgive me, your reverence, I did not observe that you were conversing with my mistress'—Eliza curtsied to the priest.—' But not a bit of it. She has treated me with marked coldness, and not so much as hinted at an invitation. It seems to me—'

'My daughter,' said the priest, 'lower your voice. We do not discuss these things so shrilly in this sacred place. Turn your thoughts to religion. Think here of your own sins, not of the shortcomings of others.'

Eliza got very red in the face.

' Believe me, I was not thinking of myself, your reverence,' she answered, quickly, ' but of my mistress. I wished to save her the expense of my dinner at the inn, by dining with my relations.—We ought to be going to the Red Horse soon, ma'am,' she added, 'or there will be no room for us.'

'Oh! but I haven't seen the stable yet,' cried little Peter, quite out loud, forgetting that he was in church. 'I don't want any dinner. But I can't go home till I have seen the stable, please.'

The little boy had jumped down off his mother's lap and stood there with the big tears in his eyes, and with the corners of his mouth quivering. It seemed to him a terrible thing to have come this long way full of expectation and hope, and then to be disappointed after all.

But the priest took his hand kindly, and led him towards the southern aisle of the church, where the crowd was, while Susan Lepage and Paul and Antony followed behind them.

'Room, my friends; have the amiability to make room,' said the priest, 'for a little lad who comes from a considerable distance to see this pious and instructive representation for the first time.'

Then little Peter felt quite proud and distinguished, for the people, at the request of the priest, moved aside to the right hand and the left, making a narrow lane for him to pass along to the gilded railings in front of the chapel, where the stable was dressed. Once there, he stood quite still, staring with very round eyes, for the sight seemed to him very beautiful and strange, and his heart was filled with wonder and awe.

In a rough, rocky cave, on the straw in a wooden manger, lay the image of the Infant Jesus, wrapped in swaddling clothes, with a golden circle above his baby head. On one side knelt the Virgin Mother, in a white robe and blue mantle, with her hands clasped meekly on her heart; and, as she bent towards her Babe, she seemed to little Peter to look at him with mild and loving eyes. On the other side stood St. Joseph, in a brown habit, leaning upon his staff. And in the dusky background the boy could just make out the form of an ass and some cows. While above the entrance of the cave shone a bright star.

'Ah, how beautiful!' said Susan Lepage softly.

'It should have been finer had we had more

money,' answered the priest with a sigh. 'Not that I complain. The parish has been generous, and the good sisters have done their best. Still, I myself greatly desired to have the Three Kings offering treasures. It would have been an effective incident—but our means are limited. They would have been too expensive for us.'

And little Peter was puzzled and could not quite comprehend what the priest meant; for he had often heard his father say that kings were old-fashioned rubbish, worth nothing at all, and that a republic was worth ten thousand of them any day in the week.

'Kneel down, my son,' said the priest to Peter presently :—' and pray to be kept pure, and innocent, and devout, so that, when your earthly warfare is accomplished—be it late or soon—you may behold the face of the Saviour in Heaven as you now behold this poor, unworthy image of Him on earth.'

Then he turned and left them.

Each of the boys bought a candle from the old woman who sat on the chapel steps, and stuck them in the round iron frame standing just by the gilded rails, and lighted them with the long taper she gave them. And Eliza bought one, too, though she was a little disposed to haggle with the old woman and accuse her of overcharging. But Susan Lepage bought three candles, and set them in the frame and lighted them. 'For,' she said, 'we must remember those who are absent—whether by choice or by misfortune—when we are in the house of God.'

CHAPTER VI.

WHICH ATTEMPTS TO SHOW WHY THE SKIES FALL.

DO you know what the snow is and where it comes from?

The Dictionary says it is 'a frozen moisture, which falls from the atmosphere in white flakes.' But that description doesn't seem to make us know very much more about it somehow.

Some people say the snow is caused by the

angels shaking the feather beds up in Heaven; but that, both scientifically and spiritually too, appears to me an improbable solution. Other people, again, say it is all the Time Spirit plucking his geese. And who are the Time Spirit's geese?—Well, if you really want to know, they are all the little poets, and little painters, and little musicians, and little players and all the little inventors of little theories, and little writers of little books, who spend their time in diligently trying to persuade themselves and others that they are great writers of great books, and discoverers of a universal panacea for the healing of the nations; and that, in short, they are not any of them geese at all, but as fine swans as you can see on any river or pond in the three kingdoms. And they come cackling, and hissing, and sidling, and waddling up to the Time Spirit every year— specially in the spring and about Christmastide—in great flocks, and all cry out together:—

'Is it possible to deny, O Time Spirit, that we are every one of us swans?'

And then, I am sorry to say—for though it is

perfectly right and just, it isn't the least bit agreeable, as some of us know to our cost—the Time Spirit turns up his sleeves and sets to work with a will, and catches them, though they mostly make a terrible noise and fluster, and plucks them one by one—big feathers first and then small—and sends them away looking sadly bare and foolish, and thereby leaving the world in no doubt whatsoever that they are only geese after all. And some wise persons, who have a perfect right to speak on the matter, think that why we have had so much more snow than usual the last few winters, is because—what with higher education and women's colleges, and one thing and another—the flocks of geese grow larger and larger, so that the poor Time Spirit is getting worn to fiddle strings with everlasting plucking, and it seems not unlikely we may soon have snowstorms nine months in the year.

But what if a real swan does come among the geese, once in a way?—Ah! that is quite another matter. For the Time Spirit discovers it in a very few minutes, and jumps up and pulls down his sleeves, and slips off his hat—he has to wear one, you know, to keep the goose down from lodging in his hair—and draws his heels together with a snap and makes a bow from the waist, like an accomplished courtier, and says :—

'All hail to you, my master or my mistress!'—as the case may be.—'For you the stars shine by night, and the sun rises at morning. All the world is yours, or shall soon be, if you have patience, and faith, and daring, and are true to the voice of the dæmon within.'

But there is yet another explanation of the snowfall besides this, and it is, perhaps, after all, the most reasonable one to believe in. For when the nights are long and the days are short, and the sunlight is feeble as a sick man's smile, the North Wind wakes from his summer sleep and calls to his brother the East Wind, and they go forth over the earth driving the heavy-laden snow-clouds before them, and the pale snow-fairies who do their will. Down from the ice floes, and the dim, silent, polar wastes, over land and sea, with a shout like the roar of a battle, and a laugh like the crackle of thunder, while the hills grow white with fear under his tread, and the forests bow themselves and shriek in his fierce breath as the planks and rigging of a ship shriek in a storm at sea, the North Wind comes. He was born hundreds of thousands of years ago, in the Ice Age, when the glaciers crawled out from the heart of the mountains, mile-long, grey-green monsters, over what are now fertile meadows and sunny plains—before man or beast, so vigorous was the keen-toothed frost, roamed over the surface of the earth. His eyes are blue and clear; and they dance as you may see the sky dance on a sharp winter's night; and his white beard hangs low on his chest, which is broad and firm as a hill-side; and he is in the full vigour of a lusty manhood still, and it promises to be a very long while yet before his eye grows dim or his limbs grow weak with age. Some think, indeed, that as he saw man first born into the world, he may live to see him die off it again—to see this great ball, which so long has been our human dwelling-place and home, rolling silent out into immeasurable space, a dead planet, locked in the arms of everlasting frost.

But be that as it may, on the fair Sunday morning, when our friend little Peter, his mother, and brothers, and Eliza, were going through the pine forest to the church at Nullepart, the North Wind was up and walking southward, southward over Europe, with the great, grey snow-clouds hurrying on before, for he had hard work to do. And, as the day wore on, he gathered the clouds from east and west, and packed them together in a vast, dusky mass over the town, and the forest and the limestone crags and gorges, and the wide, flat meadows where the cows pasture in summer, and over little Peter's home. And then he bade the snow-fairies bestir themselves, and prick the clouds as full of holes as the top of a flour-dredge, and wrap all the country in a robe of spotless white.

Now, it happened that among the snow-fairies there was one who was very young and tenderhearted. Indeed she was not really a snow-fairy at all, but a child of the soft South Wind, who, when all her sisters flew away—as the swallows fly in autumn—to the tropics, overslept herself and got left behind by mistake. And she had joined the snowfairies because she was dull and lonely, and could find no other playfellows, and nothing to do. But, for all that, she did not care to help them in their work, for she had not been brought up to it, you see, and it seemed to her a sad, chilly business. So instead of laughing and playing and flitting about, and easing the great lumbering clouds of their burden, she sat down by herself in a hollow of one of them and cried, and cried. For she could not help thinking of all the sheep on lonely hillsides; and of the small birds seeking food and finding none in the snow-buried fields, and lanes, and hedges; and of little neglected children, of whom, alas! there are always so many, in bare cottage or dreary, city cellar, with no warm clothes, or food, or firing; and of wayfarers on barren heaths and bleak moors; and of the beggars, and vagabonds, and outcasts, the sorry throng of refuse humanity, that tramps the high roads of every country of the civilised world, with neither home, nor hope, nor money, and as she thought of their frost-nipped hands, and bleeding feet, and scanty rags, she cried as if her little heart would break.

But the snow-fairies were vexed with her, and scolded and flouted her, for it is, as you all know, a great nuisance to have somebody crying and sobbing and making a fuss, when you yourselves feel quite happy and comfortable. And at last, in their irritation against her, they made such a noise and clamour, and so pushed and plagued and hustled the poor little creature, that the squabbling and commotion reached the ears of the North Wind himself, and he asked what in the name of common-sense was the matter. Then the snow-fairies all pointed at her, and all began chattering at once, as you may hear a flock of starlings chattering in the tops of the beeches at sunset, on a mild March day. But the North Wind told them to go about their business; and he took up the little fairy and stood her in the hollow of his great hand, and asked her quite gently—for the stronger a man is the gentler he can be, as you will very likely find out some fine day—why she was so sad.

Then, though she was horribly frightened and blushed up to the tips of her pretty ears, as a modest young maiden should, she looked the great North Wind bravely in the face and told him her little story—how she had been left behind, how she loved the sunshine and the summer, and how she grieved for the misery and famine that winter brings, too often, on man and bird and beast.

'And I don't see *why* it should all happen,' she said; 'or why there cannot be summer all the year.'

Still, though she spoke up so courageously, the poor, little fairy trembled, for she thought that the North Wind would be angry, as the snow-fairies had been, and that he might crush her tiny life into nothingness in the grasp of his great hand. But the North Wind did nothing of the kind. He looked at her till his clear, dancing eyes grew dim and misty; and when, at last, he spoke his voice was low and sweet and sad as church bells that the sailor hears far out at sea, as he sails at evening in sight of some fair, foreign coast.

'Ah, my child!' he said, 'all those who have once been happy, young and old, wise and foolish, mortal and immortal, mighty princes, prophets, psalmists, all living creatures, nay, the very earth herself, all that my eyes have looked on through unnumbered centuries, have asked and still ask that question in some form or other; but the answer is not granted yet. And so, knowing that till the end it may not be told us, we grow humble and grow wise; and learn that it is best to do the work that is appointed us without doubt or hesitation, careless whether it be known or unknown, pleasant or unpleasant, hard or soft, kind or cruel even, so that we get it well and honestly done. As for you, you have lost your way and have wandered from the business set for you to do, and therefore you are filled with sadness, and fears, and questionings. But have patience for a while, and have faith, too, that the mysterious purposes of the Almighty, your Master and mine, will certainly be made plain at last.—Meanwhile, go and help your cousins the snow-fairies. And then, because, though you are honest and brave, you still are frail and tender, when the night of my winter reign is over, I will give you back into the keeping of my kinsman the South Wind, who will find less sharp and cutting work for you to do.'

And all this, though you may not at first see exactly how, has a great deal to do with the story of our friend, little Peter; and therefore, even at the risk of your thinking it somewhat dry and puzzling, it has seemed to me well to set it down for you to read here.

CHAPTER VII.

WHICH DESCRIBES A PLEASANT DINNER-PARTY, AND AN UNPLEASANT WALK.

FOR when little Peter and his mother and brothers came out of the church at Nullepart, the sun had been hidden some time behind thick clouds. Fierce gusts of wind rushed down the street, blowing off hats, and blowing about petticoats, and making window-shutters rattle, and doors slam.

'Make haste, children, make haste,' cried Susan Lepage. 'We must get our dinner at the Red Horse and start homewards as quickly as we can.'

'Oh! I have been hearing something so terrible,' said Eliza, to her mistress, as she came down the church steps. 'Not that I am surprised at it—no, no, no. I have always suspected it. I am sure his appearance this morning was enough to confirm one's worst suspicions.'

Eliza pursed up her lips and shook her head with an air of extreme wisdom.

'They do say that Paqualin is a wizard,' she went on. 'Take care, Peter; if you look one way and walk another, you will unquestionably tumble down. And you needn't stare at me so. I wasn't talking to you.—Joseph Berri, the watchmaker's brother, has just been telling me all about it. There is no doubt he overlooked one of Miller Georgeon's draught oxen three years ago, so that it would not eat, and grew daily thinner and thinner, and had, at last, to be killed.—Go on, Peter; your ears will grow as long as a donkey's if you are always listening like that.—And they do say he can call up evil spirits, and storms, and thunder and lightning, and whirlwinds, when he wants them for his own vicious purposes.'

'Nonsense, Eliza, nonsense,' said Susan Lepage.

'You are far too willing to listen to idle, ill-natured tales.'

Eliza sighed profoundly and turned up her eyes.

'Ah!' she murmured, 'some day, ma'am, you will see who was in the right, and give credit where it is due. For my part, if it does snow to-day, I shall know what to think.'

'Make haste, children,' said Susan Lepage again. 'The time draws on, and we have no time to waste.'

But it was not so easy to make haste. The large dining-room of the Red Horse, with its tall, white-curtained windows, was crowded. From up the valley and down the valley in their long, narrow, country carts—for all the world like tea-trays set on four wheels—with cracking whips and jangling bells, or on foot, from lonely hamlets in the forest, or solitary herdsmen's huts on the steep grass slopes beneath the grey limestone cliffs and crags, all the inhabitants of the district had gathered to attend the church, and see the show, and spend a merry Sunday. And among all these good people were many friends of Susan Lepage, who detained her with greetings and questions. Then, too, the places at the tables were already taken, and it was some time before the boys and their mother could get seats. Even so little Peter had to squeeze himself into a very small space between Madame Georgeon,—the stout, comely wife of Monsieur Georgeon, the miller at Oùdonc—and his mother. But little Peter thought it all delightful, though he was rather pinched as to elbow-room. He liked the rattle of the knives and forks, and the many voices, and the talk and laughter; and watched with great curiosity the active serving-maids, balancing in their hands—and indeed all up their arms, too, so it seemed—an incredible number of plates and dishes. Even the floor sprinkled with sawdust, and the not altogether spotless table-cloth, were interesting. For it was all new, you see, to little Peter; and even things not very nice in themselves are charming when they are new.

Then, too, Peter was very hungry; and though Madame Georgeon's full skirts overflowed his small legs, and her handsome shawl, thrown gracefully back from her shoulders—the room was warm, what with the great, china stove in the corner and all the company—and though her shawl, I say, enveloped him entirely now and then in a cloud of many coloured cashmere, the miller's wife was very kind, and coaxed and petted him, and piled up his plate with all manner of dainty things.

'Eh, *par exemple*,' she said, smiling and nodding at him as she sipped her glass of red wine—'it is not every day we go into society, is it, to meet old friends and make new ones? You, Susan Lepage, from a child were of a serious turn of mind. That is an excellent thing, too, no doubt. It secures the future. But the present should not be despised either. The members of my family—the saints be praised—have ever possessed a little grain of gaiety in their composition. For my part I think it is only economical to make the most of this world while you are permitted to be in it. And I regard it as an actual impiety to neglect any opportunity of innocent entertainment. Eat, my child, eat then—a spoonful or so more of this admirable pastry. See, on my plate here. I was provident when the dish came round, and secured a double portion.'

Then, turning, she smiled at Susan Lepage again :—

'Do not alarm yourself. It will not injure him. He will walk it off. Exercise is a fine thing to prevent food lying heavy on the stomach.'

'Perhaps moderation is a finer one still,' answered the other gently. 'But are you not ready, my sons? We must not linger, though you in your kindness would tempt us to do so, good Madame Georgeon. We do not drive home by the high road as you do, but go on foot through the forest, and the days are short.—Antony, we should surely be moving.'

But Antony was in no haste to be going, for he, too, was making the most of this opportunity of innocent enjoyment. He sat beside Marie Georgeon, the miller's pretty daughter, who certainly took after her mother's family in respect of gaiety. And, clean glasses being somewhat scarce at the Red Horse from the unusual number of guests, it happened that she and Antony shared one; and her brown eyes were as full of mischief as a May morning is full of sunshine as she glanced up at him over the rim of it, and laughed and talked, and fingered the gold and garnet necklace that fitted so neatly about her throat. And what with her pretty looks and merry words, the young fellow's head was completely turned—and if you do not quite understand what that means, you need only wait a little, for you are bound to find out clearly enough some day. And, as the inevitable consequence of his head being turned, he hardly heard his mother when she spoke to him, and made no haste in the world to finish his dinner, and loitered and dawdled about upon one excuse and another as long as possible; and, I am sorry to say, spoke quite snappishly to his brother Paul, when the latter pointed out to him that the clock had struck three already, and that it was high time to be going. You see, it is just as well not to understand—by experience, anyhow—what it is to have your head turned, since it leads to these deplorable errors both of manners and conduct.

So it fell out that when at last our friends left the

jovial company at the Red Horse, and came out from the steaming dining-room into the street, the snow-fairies had already been some half-hour at work, and the roadway and house-roofs were all lightly powdered with snow. To little Peter, warm with his dinner, this seemed the crowning piece of fun of a glorious day. He could hardly get along for turning to look at the marks his nailed boots made in the snow. But Susan Lepage thought very differently. She glanced up at the dull, clouded sky, and remembered the sad words of John Paqualin, the charcoal-burner, that everyone had treated so lightly some few hours ago.

'Will it last, do you think?' she asked of Antony.

Antony, however, was still thinking of pretty Marie Georgeon, with whom he had shared the kernel of a double almond at parting, both wishing as they eat it. He was wishing his wish still, and it was such an agreeable one that he felt quite superior to all inconvenient incidents in the way of snowstorms and such like.—He cocked his cap more on one side than ever, and assumed quite a patronising air, even towards his mother, which, to say the least, was very silly of him.

'It may last or it may not,' he answered. ' But really, it doesn't very much matter.'

' I wish that your father was with us,' added Susan.

'Why?' cried Antony. 'He couldn't stop it snowing any more than I can. And pray remember, mother, that this isn't by any means the first time I have walked home from Nullepart in bad weather. I believe I could find my way back blindfold or at midnight for that matter.'

'I am not at all troubled about you, my son,' replied his mother quietly, ' but about our poor little Peter here, with his little short legs.'

'Oh, Peter will do well enough,' said the lad impatiently.

Some find it difficult to make room in their hearts for more than one person at a time, you know; and Antony's heart was still pretty well occupied by Marie Georgeon. He walked along briskly humming the tune of *Partant pour la Syrie*, which is a song about a young soldier who was pious as well as brave; and a lucky fellow into the bargain, for when he came back from the war he married his master the count's daughter, and lived happily ever after.

'Never mind, mother,' said Paul; 'if the snow is deep, or Peter is tired, I can carry him pick-a-back. He's not very heavy, you know.'

'I shan't be tired. I like the snow,' cried little Peter, and he clapped his hands and pranced about, till Eliza—who was still rather cross because her cousin had neglected to invite her to dinner—caught hold of him and made him walk soberly.

'If you laugh so now there will be tears before night,' she said. 'Laugh at breakfast, cry at dinner, laugh at dinner, cry at supper-time. Ah, dear me! this cold wind; I wish I had thought to put some wool in my ears—I shall be martyred with the toothache.'

So they passed down the main street. It was almost deserted now, for the storm had driven people to take shelter in the wine shops, or, which was far wiser, in their own houses. Even the pigs had gone to their styes, and the fowls to their roosts; and the goats, with their little tinkling bells, were safe housed, too, in their sheds, munching the dry, brown hay that in the summer-time had waved as green grass full of a rainbow of flowers. They passed by the smaller houses and out-buildings, and the great saw-mills where the pine logs from the mountains are cut up, that stand along the bank of the swift river; and crossed the bridge with the dark water rushing underneath; and began climbing the road that zig-zags up the long hill between the great, bare walnut-trees and stubble fields, and wild rocky pastures, to the edge of the pine forest—four tall straight figures, and one short roundabout one, showing black against the ever-deepening snow.

For, alas! the snow was falling thicker and thicker —here in the open it was already up to the second lace-hole of little Peter's boots—scurrying and racing in wild confusion before the icy breath of the North Wind; twisting, and twirling, and dancing; clinging to grass blade, and bush, and branch, and tree stem; hiding the road so that you could no longer see the margin of it; covering the wheel tracks and marks of the horse hoofs; filling up hollows under the grey rocks and boulders, and blurring the jagged outline of the pine-trees where they rise against the sky. Hundreds of thousands of

white, hurrying flakes, soft, silent multitudes, filling the air as far as eye could see. There was no fun now in turning round to look at the marks of his nailed boots, for Peter found the snow hid them again almost as soon as they were made; and it was hard work, too, struggling up the steep hill and battling with the wind.

Still the little fellow trudged along without making any complaint. For, you see, he had often heard his father praise the virtues of the Ancient Romans, their courage and endurance; and so Peter had got the notion into his head that it is rather a grand thing not to mind what is uncomfortable and disagreeable, and that it is rather a shameful and unworthy thing to grumble and make a fuss, and cry when your chilblains itch, or you happen to bump your head against the table, or when your legs ache, as his legs began to ache now, with the length and steepness of the hill. More than once his mother stopped and called him to her, and told him he was a good, brave, little man, and pulled the collar of his overcoat up about his red, little ears. And Peter, though he would not have said so for three dozen baking apples, or half a washing-basket full of sugar pigs, did find it very comfortable to stand still in the shelter of her petticoats for a minute or two and get his breath. The town below was hidden in the driving snow, and the dark wall of the pine-trees loomed nearer and nearer.

At last the forest path was reached, and here it was better walking. The snow was lighter, and there was shelter from the force of the wind. But they had taken so much time in climbing the hill that the dusk was coming on, and there was still a long way to go.

Antony no longer whistled. He walked on steadily ahead of the others, turning round now and then with a fine air of superiority and command. Antony, indeed, was as yet not at all displeased with the adventure. He believed that this was an occasion on which he showed to great advantage. His mother followed him in silence. Little Peert came next. He had taken his brother Paul's hand now, and trotted along as fast as his sturdy little legs would carry him, for to tell the honest truth he was getting a trifle frightened. The birds had all hidden themselves away in the thick brushwood, and no longer welcomed him with their merry round eyes. The well-known path looked mysterious, almost awful, in the half-light, with the tall ranks of the pine-trees on either side of it swaying in the blast. Sometimes the snow would slip in great masses from the high branches and fall close to little Peter's feet, as if the black dwarf was throwing snowballs at him. Poor Peter began to feel very shivery and creepy, and did not the least care to look round lest *something*, he did not exactly know what—and that made it all the worse, perhaps—should be coming tripping, tripping, tripping over the white ground behind him.

But the only person who really came behind little Peter was Eliza ; and though I do not want to be rude to Eliza, who was a very worthy young woman in her way, I cannot pretend to say that she was doing anything so graceful as tripping over the snow. Not a bit of it. Eliza was extremely disgruntled by the events of the day, and was as full of complaints and lamentations as a hedgehog's back is full of spines. The wet snow had made her fine, white cap limp and drabbled ; so that instead of standing up like the vizor of an ancient helmet, the big, lace frill of it tumbled in the most melancholy manner about her face. She had turned the skirt of her dress up over her head; and what with holding it, and her books tied up in her handkerchief, and what with the tightness of her boots, which were a pair of brand new ones and half a size too small for her into the bargain, Eliza came very much nearer floundering than tripping over the snow.

The forest opens out in places into wide spaces of waste moorland. Across these by daylight or in fine weather it is easy enough to find the right road; but on such an evening as I am telling you about it is by no means easy. On the edge of the moorland, Susan Lepage called to Antony to stop.

'Go slowly,' she said, 'and pray be careful. If we once mistake the path we may find ourselves in a sad plight. I wish your father was with us! Go on in front,' she added, turning to Paul, 'and I will follow you.'

Now his mother's words rather nettled Antony.

'You haven't any real confidence in me,' he said

LOST.

Page 110.

sulkily; 'or you wouldn't be repeating all the while that you wish my father was here.'

You see, Antony had been a good deal flattered and excited by his pretty companion at the Red Horse at Nullepart. And it often happens, unfortunately, that pleasure when it is past makes us quarrelsome. He kicked the snow about with his foot, and his handsome, young face looked quite rebellious and naughty.

'No, no, my son,' Susan Lepage answered gently. 'I have every confidence in your good intentions. But the way must needs be difficult to find. I merely caution you to be careful.'

'Of course I shall be careful,' said the lad angrily, as he stepped from the shelter of the pine trees into the dim, white waste beyond.

For a time all went well; but, all of a sudden, the ground began to grow rough and uneven under foot. Peter stumbled and fell, and scrambled up again half smothered in snow, his poor, little mouth and eyes full of it, and his hands scratched with the harsh heath roots and stones beneath.

'Antony, Antony, we are wandering!' cried his mother, as she wiped the snow out of Peter's eyes and off his clothes, and kissed him. The little boy clung to her, for he felt very desolate and cheerless. He did not think it in the least amusing now to be out in the storm. He longed for the warm, cosy kitchen and for the society of Cincinnatus; but he choked down his tears as his mother kissed him, and tried to be very brave and not to mind his tumble.

Antony turned back, he was a few steps ahead.

'We can only have missed the path by a yard or two,' he said hurriedly. 'You just stand still and I'll find it.'

And he did find it. But, alas! he could not keep to it, for the light faded and darkness came on quicker and quicker, and still the snow fell in hundreds of thousands of soft white flakes. Eliza groaned and lamented, and our poor, little Peter's snow-clogged boots began to chill his feet through, and his hands grew as cold as frogs' paws, and he got more and more hungry and tired. But he did not grumble about it, for he knew his mother and brothers were cold and weary too; so he struggled on manfully through the ankle-deep snow. And, at last, he got too tired even to feel hungry, and began to cry quite gently to himself.

'Please, mother,' he said, 'I can't go any further.'

Susan Lepage took him up in her arms and held

him close against her bosom. She did not speak; but, if it had been light enough to see, I think Peter would have found that she was crying too. For the ground was all rough and uneven under foot again; and though Antony went first to the right hand and then to the left he could not make out the road at all.

'I've come all wrong, mother,' he said, and his voice trembled. 'I don't know where we are or which way we are walking. We are lost.'

There was a silence before his mother answered him.

'You have done your best,' she said. 'The event is in the hands of God.'

CHAPTER VIII.

WHICH PROVES THAT EVEN PHILOSOPHIC POLITICIANS MAY
HAVE TO ADMIT THEMSELVES IN THE WRONG.

BUT now it is quite time for us to go back to the old, wooden farm-house on the edge of the forest, and see what Master Lepage, and Gustavus, and that intelligent and experienced person, Cincinnatus, are doing, while the rest of the household are wandering, alas! not without growing alarm, and even suffering, in the darkness and cold and snow.

In point of fact, then, though Master Lepage had been so very determined to please himself by sitting at home, he had found the day uncommonly long and dull. For he was one of those sociable persons who are never quite happy without an audience to hold forth to and instruct, and convince of their own remarkable wisdom and the hearers' equally remarkable folly. And then, too, for all that he appeared somewhat dictatorial and highhanded, Lepage was at bottom an affectionate and warm-hearted man, who loved his wife and children tenderly. And so, as the afternoon drew on, and the wind rose and the clouds gathered, he began to get into a fine fume and fret. He walked up and down the warm, cosy kitchen as restless as a bear in a pit; and knocked double postman's knocks on the weather glass, and declared out loud that the mercury was going up, when he saw perfectly well that it was going down; and did a number of other useless things to try to persuade himself that he was not one bit anxious or uneasy.

'How inferior is the education of men to that of cats!' thought Cincinnatus. 'Before I was old enough to lap milk out of a saucer, my mother had taught me the vulgarity of giving way to purposeless agitation. "Calm," she would say, "is even a greater sign of good-breeding than a curl of hair inside the ears." In my poor master, there, calm and ear-curls alike are wanting. What a situation! Thank heaven, I at least was born a cat!'

But, you see, Master Lepage had really some cause for his restlessness, for all this while he was struggling with an unseen enemy. Deep down in that innermost chamber of the heart—the door of which we most of us keep so tight shut because we know Truth sits within weighing and judging all our thoughts and actions, and letting us know from time to time just what she thinks about them in the very plainest language—in that innermost heart-chamber, I say, Lepage was aware that there was a busy, active feeling of shame and remorse. And while Truth pushed hard at the door inside to let the Feeling out, he pushed equally hard on the outside to keep the Feeling in. But when finally the snow began to fall, and the daylight lessen, and the storm grow fierce and fiercer, Truth pushed and bumped and banged upon the poor door so unmercifully that Master Lepage, sturdy veteran though he was, grew quite weary of opposing her. And so the busy Feeling popped out first its head, and then its two arms, and then squeezed itself out all together, and began racing up and down the whole length and breadth of the old soldier's heart in the most audacious manner.

'You were obstinate and conceited this morning,' said the Feeling; 'you wouldn't listen to John Paqualin, the charcoal-burner. Look at the snow!'

'The glass was rising,' answered Lepage. 'I am perfectly certain it was. And John Paqualin is a madman.'

'Madman yourself,' said the Feeling—for feelings are very free-spoken, you know, and don't mince matters—'madman yourself for letting your wife, who is a delicate woman, and that poor child, little Peter, run such a risk of cold, and fatigue, and perhaps worse.'

'Antony knows the way,' answered Lepage again. 'And he's an able fellow.'

'He is a boy, and like most boys is thoughtless and self-opinionated. He takes after you in that last, by the same token,' said the Feeling.

'I am a philosophic politician,' cried Lepage, somewhat hotly. 'I worship the goddess of Reason.'

'Do you?' said the Feeling. 'And these newspapers you were so anxious to sit at home and read to-day, full—as you perfectly well know—of garbled news, and one-sided statements, and of cheap party cries—they are the voice of Reason, are they?'

'Hang you!' answered Lepage—which was not at all a pretty way of answering. But then, you see, poor Master Lepage was getting very angry because he was very uncomfortable; and when persons are both uncomfortable and angry they are liable to make use of expressions which, very properly, are *not* printed in the French and English conversation books that you study in the schoolroom.—'I won't listen to you. So away with you. I have no doubt—'

'No doubt, haven't you?' said the Feeling. 'Well, I am glad to hear that.'

'No doubt at all—ten thousand plagues on you—

no doubt at all, I say, that my wife and children will be home in ten minutes at the latest. Meanwhile I will read a little. I will improve my mind with the history of those grand, old Romans.'

So Lepage got down the history book, and it fell open at one of his favourite passages—the account of the Consul, Marcus Attilius Regulus, who, rather than break his word, left his home and kindred and gave himself up to his pitiless enemies, and bore in silence all the cruel tortures to which they subjected him.

'There was a man!' cried Lepage, as he wiped his spectacles with his red pocket-handkerchief.

'Yes, indeed, a very different man to you, Francis Louis Lepage,' said the Feeling.

'Why, why what do you mean? Twenty thousand cut-throat Prussians!—at least I am no coward. No one has ever accused me of that before. What was I ever afraid of?'

'Of a little trouble,' answered the Feeling. 'Of a walk, for instance, when you felt inclined to sit at home smoking—of what one or two silly, feather-headed

WAITING.

Page 120.

fellows, who fancy themselves mighty sharp and clever, might perhaps say about you, if you were seen kneeling down beside your wife and sons, in the church there, with your head uncovered, praying God to forgive you your sins.—Pooh, don't talk about your courage to me!' said the Feeling.

Master Lepage sat very still for some time after that in the window-seat, with the Roman History wide open before him; but he did not care to go on reading about the Consul Regulus. He remembered how little Peter had climbed on his knee on Friday evening, and coaxed him to go to Nullepart to see the Infant Jesus and the stable; and had said —poor, little lad, what a nice, little face he had— Lepage rubbed the end of his hooked nose, and sniffed—that if only his father came with them they would all be so happy.

'Well, I hope they have been happy,' he said to himself. 'It is more than I have been, in any case.'

He turned and looked out of window. Ah! how it snowed, and how dark it was growing.

'And with this wind, on the moorland the snow will drift. If they have the intelligence of a blue owl between them they will have started early!'

he cried quite fiercely. 'Ten thousand plagues— poor dear souls,' he added, for Master Lepage was getting a little confused somehow.

He hurried across the kitchen to the house-door

and flung it wide open, and standing on the threshold, gazed long and earnestly down the dim forest path, drawing his shaggy eyebrows together till they stood out like *chevaux de frise* above his keen, grey eyes.

'Ho-la, ho-la, hey!' he shouted. But there was no answer save the roaring of the wind among the pines and the soft 'hush, hush,' of the falling snow.

Now for some time past Cincinnatus had been sitting very composedly staring with his great, yellow eyes into the glowing log fire, and meditating pleasantly on the inferiority of men to cats. But when Master Lepage, a prey to that remorseful Feeling which Truth had let loose to tramp where it would up and down his heart, threw the house-door wide open, the icy breath of the North Wind rushed wildly into the kitchen, and made our friend Cincinnatus feel uncommonly cool about the back.

'Neither calm nor ear-curls, dear me!' he murmured to himself as he rose slowly, stretching one fore leg and then the other, and then each hind leg in turn — shaking the last leg rapidly for a moment, too, because it was slightly cramped—and yawning the while so wide, that his pink tongue was curled up quite tight, like a rolling-pin, at the back of his mouth. Then he moved away with dignity, intending to take up his station upon the cushion of the big arm-chair that stood in the corner nicely out of the draught. But all of a sudden Cincinnatus heard something that made him jump all on one side with an arched back and a bristling tail, and say 'Pffzsh!' twice over, as loud as ever he had said it in his life.

It was an unfamiliar sound that so startled Cincinnatus, for Master Lepage was pulling strongly at the rope of the big bell that hung under the centre gable of the old house, and the urgent clang of its iron voice rang through the thick, snow-laden air far over the forest. The bell had been placed there long years before to summon neighbours—the house standing in a solitary place—in case of fire or accident. And now Lepage rang it with a double purpose, trusting that even if its friendly tones failed to reach the ears of the poor wanderers, it might at least bring Gustavus, the cowherd, from his father's cottage on the edge of the pastures, where he was spending the Sunday, and that he might help him search for the wife and children whom he loved so well.

'By my great-grandmother's whiskers!' exclaimed Cincinnatus, as he settled himself down on the chair cushion, 'what with draughts, and bell-ringing, and one thing and another, this house will soon be impossible for a cat of any pretensions to gentility. Compare it with the Sacristan's establishment, now, where you can't tell one day from another except by the smell of the different soups for dinner.—Delightful!—With an occasional vocal evening, too, in the back garden, when the moon is full. Lots are strangely unequal in this world!—Pffzsh! and to add to everything else, if there actually is not that intolerable charcoal-burner.'

John Paqualin stood on the threshold, a flaming torch of pine boughs in his hand; his long, unkempt hair was white with snow, and so was the tattered cloth cloak that hung in so many folds from his stooping shoulders. His eyes were bright and glowing.

'Ah! the wind,' he said, 'the glorious wind, the roar and the shout of it; the cry of the trees that strain, and the passionate snap of the branches—like heart-strings that snap under the blast of incurable sorrow. And the snow, soft and pure, and light as the coverlet a young mother lays on her first-born's cradle—getting a little too thick just now, though, that coverlet.—Eh! what's this? have you smothered the infant—laid it over the face as well? Be careful, then, with your—But the bell,' he added suddenly, interrupting himself, and catching hold of Master Lepage with his hard, thin fingers—' it called to me, while I was listening to the roll of the drums, and the blare of the trumpets, and the scream of the fifes in the forest there, and made me come hither whether I would or no. What do you want spoiling all my splendid wind-music with your infernal bell-clatter?'

'Want!' cried Lepage hoarsely; 'I want help.'

Paqualin laughed aloud.

'Hey-ho,' he said. 'Times are changed, are they? I never heard you sing that song before.'

Lepage let go the bell-rope, and raised his clenched fist. But he did not strike the blow. Something stopped him. Perhaps it was that same remorseful Feeling which Truth had let loose in his heart.

'Come inside, Paqualin,' he said quite quietly, after a moment or two. 'Now try to remember.—My wife and sons and our maid-servant went to church at Nullepart this morning. You did your best to prevent them going. You said the snow was coming, and it has come. They should have been back a good two hours ago, and they are not here yet.'

'Not here yet,' repeated the charcoal-burner slowly.

'No, not yet.' Lepage drew his hand across his eyes. 'Would to God,' he said, 'I had gone along with them.—But see now, I will light the lamp and leave the house-door open; and then will go out to search for them. You can find your way like a hound, they say, by night or day, through the forest. Will you come with me and help me?'

Paqualin stood in front of the fire; the snow on his hair and cloak melted and ran down, forming a little pool of water about his ill-shod feet.

'I am not over and above fond of you, Francis Lepage,' he said presently, 'as you most likely know already. Love and hatred alike can tell their own story without much need of spoken words. I think you a vain man and a hard one; but your wife is as pitiful as the saints in heaven. You want me to help you to find her? You have not got a dog to do the work for you, and so you'll take me. Ah, well! I've known the dog's place pretty well all my life long; —the kicks and the cuffs, and the grudging crust from the master's table; and then the " Here! my good fellow, good cur, here! nose down, tail up, the scent's cold, but still you're sharp enough to find it; and sweat and faint to catch the hare that will make your owner a savoury supper, while you slink home to the dirty straw and the mouldy crust again." Yes, yes—to be sure, I'll go with you and find them and bring them home; your fair wife and your children, and leave you happy and go back to my hut and the voices—not for your sake though, mind you, but for hers—the only woman whose eyes have ever looked kindly upon me.'

'Come on your own terms,' said Lepage.

Just then Gustavus, in his heavy boots, came clumping into the kitchen.

'The bell, master—has the red cow calved of a sudden?' he asked. For once in his life Gustavus appeared to be quite excited. He forgot to take off his hat or put down his big cotton umbrella, from off which the wet snow slipped in little avalanches, *sthlop*, on to the floor.

'Calf thyself, with thy great, stupid, cheese face!' cried the charcoal-burner.

Then while Lepage gave the cowherd his orders, and got some things together to take with them, Paqualin stood murmuring to himself, with his head bent low, and his lean, grimy hands stretched out towards the comfortable blaze of the fire:—

'You, the man, welcome, and brave, and beloved. I, the dog, to show the man the way. Gustavus, there, the ass, to trot behind loaded up with the

blankets, and the food, and the brandy. And in the end, what? A bone for the dog, a thistle for the ass, and for the man kisses. Which has the best of it? Hardly fair, is it, eh?'

'Umph,' said Gustavus, as he got the big bundle on to his back. 'Perhaps she'll be a bit soft-hearted when she sees me. Maybe the snow will have taken some of the starch out of our Eliza.'

CHAPTER IX.

WHICH IS VERY SHORT, BECAUSE, IN SOME WAYS, IT IS RATHER SAD.

HAVE you ever looked for something you cared for very much and failed to find it? A dolly, for instance, forgotten at play in the garden, swept up with the dead leaves, and never seen after. Or, still worse, a dear little kitten of an adventurous turn of mind, that went out in the woods for a walk by himself and never came home again, though you ran down the church-lane and up to the top of the pasture, crying, ' Puss, puss, puss!' till you were quite hoarse, and cross, and tired, and nurse said you must come in because it was past bed-time and the dew was rising, and a number of other things which were perfectly true, but which didn't throw any light on the whereabouts of the kitten. How did you feel? Why, just the most miserable little boy or girl in all the world, to be sure.

Or supposing, on the other hand, that you found dolly at last, after all; but with all the red washed off her lips and cheeks, and the mould mixed up with her yellow hair, and her smart frock wet and torn, and one of her waxen legs squashed flat where the wheel of the gardener's barrow had gone over it. Or that the keeper brought back poor kitty some three or four days later, stiff and cold, and said :—' Bin poaching, bin caught in a gin; thought little missy 'ud like to know the end of 'er.' Well, did that make matters much better? I don't think so myself, and at one time of my life I had a good deal of experience in these things, so I have the right to speak. For it is a poor pleasure at best to play that dolly is sick of a fever, when you see that she does not get a bit better, even though you dose her ten times a day with an elaborate preparation of slate-pencil scrapings. And as to begging a candle-box of the housemaid for a coffin, and having a grand funeral in the shrubbery for the kitten, that is terrible work indeed, and makes your eyes so red with crying that you are quite ashamed to go down to dessert in the evening.

Now, if you and I have felt so very unhappy over our dolls and kittens when we lost them—and found them again, maybe, but always a good deal the worse for the losing—how do you think Master Lepage felt as he went out that dark, stormy, snowy night, with the charcoal-burner and Gustavus, into the forest? He was very silent as he tramped through the snow, while the wind roared in the pines above him, and blew about the flame of his torch, making it twist and twirl, and flicker and glimmer, sometimes casting a red glare far over the white ground and the great, grey tree-stems and John Paqualin's crooked, uncouth form flitting on just ahead of him; and sometimes dying down till all the scene was wrapped in darkness. He was very silent, I say, and not a bit like vivacious, loquacious Master Lepage who used to sit and hold forth in the wine-shop, and thump the table and make the glasses ring; but more like Sergeant Lepage, who, with his teeth set and his face fierce and white, had marched up under fire of the enemies' guns in battle long ago in Italy or Africa. Lepage marched under fire now, and the battlefield was his own heart. And oh! dear me, how many of his most cherished ideas and beliefs the shot from those guns knocked over—his pride, his self-importance, his trust in his own intellect and insight and acuteness, his politics, his philosophy; nothing, in short, nothing was left standing, except a sense of remorse for his past folly and his love for his wife and his children.

'If they have been merely delayed by the storm, we shall meet them on the road here. If they are lost, they will have begun wandering on the first stretch of moorland,' said John Paqualin. 'See, the snow is ceasing, the stars begin to show in heaven. Eh! the frost, how it bites!'

And so it did. As the snow stopped, the night grew colder and colder, for all the ice-fairies came tripping out far and wide over hill and valley, and built transparent piers and bridges across the streams and pools, and hung icicles from the rocks and from the overhanging eaves of the houses, and froze the breath on Lepage's long moustache, and made the earth like iron beneath his feet. Yet he and his two companions still marched on through the forest. They could go but slowly, for in the open spaces the snow had drifted deep, and where the forest paths crossed each other it required all the charcoal-burner's knowledge and skill to tell which was the right one. Now and again they would halt for a minute or two and call aloud, and then listen hoping for an answer; but it was close upon midnight, and they had walked more than half the way to Nullepart before they came upon any trace of those they so earnestly searched for.

Here, as I have already told you, the path crosses a wide stretch of rolling moorland, covered with heather and stunted bushes, thorns and brambles and whortle-berry and juniper; while in places crop out large limestone blocks and boulders, some standing together and looking like the ruins of a giant's castle, others but just peeping above the rough soil and encrusted with stone-crop, and ferns and many kinds of mosses—a lovely play-place on a summer day, when the butterflies sport over the heath, and the dragon-flies over the pools in the marshes, but bleak and desolate enough on a December night, with the harsh north wind and the snowstorm. On the edge of this moorland, before leaving the shelter of the pines, Paqualin stopped.

'Shout,' he said, turning to the others, 'shout your loudest. The frost has caught me by the throat, and squeezed my crooked windpipe till I am as hoarse as a raven. But you are strong men. Shout, Lepage, for love of your wife. And you, good ass, there, for love of Eliza your sweetheart; she'll pay you in thistles, prickles and all, if you find her.'

So they shouted, and this time there was an answer—a boy's voice half choked with crying. And with a pale, haggard face, and in his eyes a look of terror, from among the snow-laden pine-trees, came Antony.

'You alone!' cried Lepage. 'I trusted her to you; where are your mother and brothers?'

'She sent us on to try to get help. Paul is here just behind me. We lost ourselves, and wandered. She could get no further, and little Peter is dead asleep, under the big rocks, there to the right, out on the moor. Eliza does nothing but cry, and won't move.'

The boy was utterly faint and disheartened. He threw himself down on the snow, and covered his face with his hands.

'I did my best, father,' he said, 'indeed, indeed I did; but I couldn't find the way. It was dark, and there was nothing to guide us, and I got bewildered with the cold. We were too late in starting, I know—that was my fault. But I did my best afterwards. Oh! father, I did try to take care of them. I couldn't help it. Say you forgive me.'

Paqualin did not wait to hear more. 'The big rocks out to the right,' he repeated.

His limbs were stiff with the sharp cold, which

FOUND. Page 138.

had penetrated his threadbare clothes, and his feet were numb with the snow that had worked its way in through the worn, cracked leather of his wretched boots. Oh, yes! I am afraid he was a very funny figure indeed ; and that all the little boys in Nullepart would have hooted louder than ever if they could have seen him, as with his long grasshopper legs, wild red hair, and tattered cloak streaming out behind him, he shambled along, slipping and staggering, in the half darkness over that long halfmile of heath, and stone, and prickly bushes, and sly, deceitful snow-drifts that stretched between the edge of the forest and the rocks.

'Here is help,' he shrieked in his shrill voice. 'It is I—I, John Paqualin. Here is help.'

As he passed round in front into the shelter of the tall, grey rocks, Susan Lepage rose up from the foot of them with a great cry.

She flung her arms about him, and rested her fair head on his shoulder.

'Ah! God has sent you,' she sobbed. 'I called upon Him in the bitterness of my anguish, and He has heard me. Save us, John Paqualin; in mercy save me and my children.'

The charcoal-burner's torch slipped from his grasp, and fell hissing upon the ground.

'The dog gets something more than his bone for once,' he said between his teeth.

For a minute or so, in that mysterious, ghostly radiance of dancing star-light and white snow, he stood holding the weeping woman in his arms.

'God sent me, though, did He?' he murmured at last. 'Then I must do His good pleasure, not my own.'

Paqualin spoke low, and quite softly, notwithstanding that queer crack in his voice.

'Look up, and take courage; there is better comfort than mine at hand. Your two boys are safely cared for already, and your husband is coming. The trouble is over. For you, at least, the morning begins to break.'

Then, as he heard the crunch of hurried footsteps coming over the snow behind him, he turned and cried:—

'Here, take your wife, Lepage!'

Paqualin moved aside.

'For the man,' he said, half aloud—'well—what he's a right to. Get back to your kennel, you hound.'

Now Eliza was sitting with her back against one of the rocks in the burrow, where the snow was lightest, and little Peter, closely wrapped in his mother's shawl, lay stupefied with sleep, with his head in her lap. As Paqualin turned round, she moaned out:—

'No, no, don't come near me. I am dreadfully ill—probably I shall never recover. I think I shall die. But I won't give way, I won't listen to you. To the last I am true to Gustavus. Ah! my poor heart, how it beats. Yes, I should like to have bidden a last farewell to Gustavus.'

'Don't fret,' answered the charcoal-burner. 'Thy mooncalf is on the road. He'll be here in plenty of time to say a good deal besides good-bye to you, unless I am very much mistaken.'

Eliza gave a prodigious sigh.

'He will be too late, I know it, I know it. Ah! how will he live without me, poor, faithful, broken-hearted Gustavus?'

Whether it was his mother's cry that roused him, or the sudden lights and the voices, I do not know; but little Peter half awoke from the heavy torpor of sleep into which the cold and fatigue had plunged him.

'I will not hush, Eliza. I love John Paqualin. Yes, I love him,' he murmured.

CHAPTER X.

WHICH ENDS THE STORY.

'SOMETHING has gone very wrong,' said Cincinnatus to himself in the cat language. 'I don't pretend to understand it. This is one of those many matters that I should be glad to take my cousin the Sacristan's cat's opinion upon. Dear me! what a misfortune it is to live here in the country, away from the centre of social intercourse and civilisation.'

Then Cincinnatus fell to washing his face with his paws, for he had lately had his five o'clock saucer of milk, you see; and it is etiquette in cat-land always to wash after meals, not before them as we do.

The yellow earthenware stove was lighted in the bedroom, and Cincinnatus sat opposite to the open door of it, and blinked at the heart of crimson wood embers, set in a fringe of flaky, grey ashes. It was very warm there, but Cincinnatus blinked and washed his face slowly. As to the heat, it soothed him, and inclined him to make a number of reflections.

'At the risk of repeating myself, I must observe that men are poor, improvident, thoughtless creatures,' he went on presently; 'subject to illness and accidents of all kinds. However, a thoughtful cat will not be hard upon them. *Noblesse oblige.* Those who have the advantage can afford to be generous. Fancy coming into this world, now, where the weather is so extremely uncertain, all pink and bare as they do, poor things, without any comfortable fur to cover them; and having to make up for it by enclosing themselves in all sorts of shapeless, foreign substances, prepared from sheep's wool or vegetables. And no tail either! Imagine being deprived of that most dignified and expressive member. Yet, you must give them their due.

Necessity has certainly made them very ingenious.'

Cincinnatus stretched himself lazily in the hot glow of the stove fire.

'But with all their ingenuity only one life,' he said yawning. 'And that one, as I observed just now, subject to all manner of illness and accident. We have nine lives! Who would be one of them if he could help it? Poor things, no wonder if they envy us.'

Then Cincinnatus went across the boarded floor with his noiseless tread, and jumped up on to little Peter's bed, and began purring in the most amiable and engaging manner, sticking out all his claws and then drawing them in again and making a nice tight little fist, as he trampled on the bed-clothes, first with one fore-foot and then with the other. He even went so far as to rub his head along against the little boy's shoulder, which, considering his opinion of the relative position of cats and mankind in the universal scale of being, was really very condescending of him, to my thinking.

L

But little Peter did not speak or pay any attention to Cincinnatus. He only sighed in his sleep, and turned his round, black head on the pillow. Poor little Peter had lain just like that, quite still and quiet, in bed ever since his father and the charcoal-burner had placed him there when they had got home from that terrible walk in the snow, about four o'clock in the morning. The ice-fairies, who really are very elegant people and not at all disagreeable when you know them, had come at sunrise and spread the most beautiful patterns—crowns and crosses, and stars and diamonds, and ice flowers of a hundred exquisite shapes—all over the window panes; but little Peter had been too tired and sleepy to get up and look at them. And when, in the afternoon, not without struggle and difficulty, for the road was dangerous with snow-drifts, the kind, old doctor, with his red nose and his snuffbox, had ridden over from Nullepart, and sat by the little boy's bed and felt his pulse, and examined him carefully, with a face as wise as an owl's, from behind his large spectacles, Peter had been too tired and sleepy to look at him either. The old doctor had taken an extra pinch of snuff, and shaken his head quite seriously, I am sorry to say, at leaving.

Now it was past five o'clock, and Peter still lay in his little bed dozing and sleeping—dreaming too, but not of the snow and the pain of the winter. He dreamed of sunshine and of pleasant places, of the singing of birds and the sound of the cow-bells in the flowery fields in the spring-time. The elder boys and their father had gone to see the doctor safe part of his way home again. And Susan Lepage had sunk down in the big chair in the kitchen, and had fallen asleep, worn out with fatigue and anxiety. And Eliza, hearing Gustavus come into the back kitchen with the milk-pans, had slipped downstairs from watching beside the child, just to have a word with him.

'Poor fellow,' she said, 'he really is so overjoyed at my being restored to him, that there is no saying if he won't mix this evening's milk with this morning's, or ruin the cream by shaking it, or commit some other folly. He is not clever, and my family will certainly reproach me with having married beneath me; but he has a good heart, and I think he really appreciates me as he ought to, does Gustavus.'

So it happened that little Peter was left quite alone, but for the society of the cat, up in the bedroom.

John Paqualin came along the flagged path to the front of the house; and pressing his face close against the glass, for it was difficult to see through them, the panes being frosty, looked in at the kitchen window. Then he went to the house door, lifted the latch carefully, entered, and stood still, listening. There was no sound save the singing of the kettle, and Eliza's chatter in the distant dairy, with the clump of the cowherd's boots on the flags and the clink of the milk-pans. From the rows of copper kettles and saucepans, and the china high on the dresser, to the red tiled floor under the charcoal-burner's feet, the large kitchen actually shone with exquisite cleanliness. The light of the lamp on the table fell upon Susan Lepage's high, white cap, showing it and her pure, grave profile, as she leaned her head back in the arm-chair,

clear cut against the ruddy dusk of the chimney corner behind her.

Paqualin, as he stood there silent and watchful, with his sunken eyes, ungainly figure, and dilapidated garments, seemed strangely out of place. He shaded his eyes with his hand, for the light dazzled him, as he looked for a minute or two at the sleeping mother. Then he went quietly across the kitchen and up the wide, wooden staircase.

'The house is asleep,' he murmured in his high, cracked tones :—' or would be but for the voice of Eliza. Pah! the woman's tongue cuts like a whip. But her sweetheart, the ass, has a good thick hide of his own; he finds the lash only pleasantly tickling.'

Paqualin went into the warm, dimly-lighted bedroom above.

'The house is asleep,' he repeated. 'Hey-ho, Sleep's a kindly fellow, with his turban of nodding poppies. He cures the heart-ache. But he's forgetful, sadly forgetful. He hasn't been near me these five nights; and God knows, I have had the heart-ache as badly as any of the others.'

He knelt down by little Peter's bed, and looked closely at the child.

'Eh! Sleep is hardly a kind friend to you, I'm afraid, though,' he said under his breath. 'A little

THE CHARCOAL-BURNER VISITS LITTLE PETER.

Page 130.

too much of the smell of the drowsy poppies here to be quite healthful.'

As he spoke, Cincinnatus, who had been curled up comfortably in a nice, warm depression in the bed-clothes, jumped down on to the floor with glaring eyes and a great tail.

'I won't spit though,' he said. 'It really isn't worth the trouble. No, an air of absolute indifference will be even more impressive and chilling.'

So he walked away very stiffly, and sat down opposite the open stove door again.

The charcoal-burner placed one of his lean hands on the little boy's soft, pudgy one, that lay palm upward on the pillow, and with the other patted him tenderly on the cheek.

'Little Peter,' he said, 'wake up. Come back to us, dear, little mouse. You said you loved me— nobody ever said that to me before. Don't go away from me, do not desert me.'

He paused a minute, and then went on pleadingly :—

'Think of all the stories I have told you, remember the nuts and the apples.—Eh! wake up, little lad, and come back to poor, ugly John Paqualin, to whom his fellow men have shown such scant mercy.'

But the child lay quite still; his long, black eyelashes resting on his pale cheeks, and his pretty, round mouth a wee bit open as he sighed softly in that strange stupor of sleep.

Tears dimmed the charcoal-burner's eyes. He bent his wild shock head and rested it down on the white coverlet.

'Ah, great God!' he murmured, 'Thou who art all powerful, listen to me. See here, can't we make an exchange?—Take my poor, battered, weary, old soul instead of his fresh, innocent, white one. Let me give him my life for his mother's sake, the sweetest and most compassionate of women. She will grieve if she loses him, her darling, her baby; and kind as she is, she won't miss me very much. Why should she?—an outcast of nature, a shameful, misshapen mistake; one sorry sight the less in the world when I'm gone, that's all.—Death's dreadful, they say—yes, I know I am afraid of it. But, after all, it can't be so very much worse than life—at least for some of us.'

He threw back his head, and clasped his hard hands together.

'Here, take me,' he cried. 'I will come. A trifle of suffering, more or less, what does it matter? Spare the little lamb, O Lord, and take me, John Paqualin, as ransom.'

Now the charcoal-burner was not quite right in his head, you see, and that accounts for his eccentric prayer and very original behaviour. You had better bear this in mind. I won't tell you why; you will probably find out for yourselves when you have seen more of the world and grown rather older.

Paqualin knelt on there for some time, looking up as though he expected a direct and visible answer to his singular petition. But nothing happened save that Eliza came upstairs on the tips of her toes—a way of stepping which she intended to be particularly quiet, but which was, in fact, particularly noisy—and peeped into the room. Seeing the charcoal-burner kneeling by the bed-side, she gave a fearful gasp, and sank down into the nearest chair.

'The saints help and preserve us!' she exclaimed in a loud whisper, holding her side, 'what next? Ah! how it startled me. The helpless, sick child in the arms of that ogre! Go away, John Paqualin, go away. How on earth did you get here? I've only been downstairs three minutes giving some necessary instructions to Gustavus.—He really is beside himself with joy, poor fellow.—Go away, I say; if Peter woke up suddenly he would have a fit at seeing you. Look at yourself in the looking-glass, and you'll understand why, fast enough. A rush of blood to the head from fright and the child would be dead. And if half the stories one hears of you are true, there is enough down on the wrong side of your account already without adding wilful murder. Go along with you.—Ah! I am so weak—my poor heart, how it beats.'

Eliza advanced, creaking across the boarded floor, towards the charcoal-burner. He had risen to his feet.

'There is no answer,' he said, in a low voice. 'You fool, learn your lesson. God doesn't want your wretched, worthless soul, John Paqualin. Who are you, indeed, that you should try to strike a bargain with the Almighty, and offer such miserable refuse and offscourings as your life in place of that of the pure and sinless child there?'

He looked back towards the bed.

'Good-bye,' he said, 'dear, little Peter. When you are gone there will be nothing left on earth to love me; and in heaven it's clear they can do very well without me yet awhile.'

Then, as Eliza came close to him, whispering, pointing towards the door, and signing to him, he turned upon her with a terrible face.

'Woman, leave me alone,' he said. 'Have not I enough to bear already, without the maddening gnat-bites of your spiteful ignorance and cruel folly?'

And the grasshopper man went out of the room, and down the stairs, and into the dark frosty night.

Eliza leant up against the bottom of the bed, with her eyes half shut.

'Are you gone yet,' she murmured, 'you savage, wild animal?—If the child had woke up and screamed there would have been a fine fuss, and all the blame would have been laid on me, of course. It isn't fair that crazy men like that should be allowed to persecute respectable, young servant-women. I'll get Gustavus to lay an information against him at the police station at Nullepart for using threatening language to me. Of course it is all jealousy; but I can't help my good looks.'

Eliza opened her eyes again, arranged the mauve silk handkerchief about her neck, and smiled complacently.

'It is a comfort to know that you have no cause to be ashamed of your face—or of your disposition, for that matter, either,' she added.

Now this all happened on Monday evening, as no doubt you have made out already. Very early, before it was light on Wednesday morning, little Peter, who all that long time had lain sleeping unconscious of what went on around him, suddenly seemed to find himself very wide awake indeed. There was a strange light in the room, bright and yet soft like an early summer dawn. And as the little boy opened his eyes, he saw that at his bedside there stood a young man, with a calm, beautiful face and shining hair. He was clothed down to the feet in a long, white, linen garment.

As Peter looked up wonderingly, the young man bent over him. There was something very still and gentle in his glance, and the little boy smiled, for it seemed to him that the young man's face was that of an old friend, though he could not remember ever to have seen him before.

Then the young man spoke to him, and said:—

'Little Peter, you have been sick and tired. Will you come away with me to a far-off country where there is no more sickness and trouble, and where the children play all the year round among blooming flowers in green, sunny pastures by the riverside?'

Peter did not feel a bit afraid; but he thought of his parents and his brothers, and asked:—

'But, please, will my mother, and father, and Paul, and Antony, and my cat Cincinnatus, come too? Paul is very kind, and he makes such nice mill-wheels to turn in the brook, and weathercocks to stick up in the pear-tree and show which way the wind blows. And Cincinnatus would be dull and lonely if I left him behind. He likes to come to bed with me in the morning, and the old grey wolf might come out of the wood and catch him, and make him into soup for little wolves when I was gone.'

The young man smiled as he answered:—
'Never fear. Your mother and father and Paul and Antony will certainly join you some day if they are good. Time seems very short while we wait in that happy country. And as to Cincinnatus, who knows but that he may come also? In any case, he will be quite safe, for our Heavenly Father loves all his living creatures—not only angels and men, but fish, and birds, and beasts as well. Will you come, little Peter?'

'Ah! but there's John Paqualin,' said the boy. 'You know whom I mean—the charcoal-burner. I can't leave him very well, you see, because he is often very unhappy; and he says nobody will ever care for him because he is rather odd and ugly-looking. And I do care for him very much indeed.'

Then the young man bent lower and looked into little Peter's eyes.

'Why, why you are John Paqualin!' cried the child.

'Yes,' said the other, and his face was radiant with the peace that passes understanding. 'I am John Paqualin. God be praised.'

'But how you have changed!' little Peter said; for he was a good deal surprised, you know, and no wonder.

'With the Lord one day is as a thousand years,' answered the young man. 'Will you come with me now, little Peter?'

Then Peter stretched out his hands and laughed out loud with joy; he was so very glad about quite a number of things—the thought of his playfellows in that fair and happy country, and of the coming of his parents and brothers, and of Cincinnatus the cat, and most of all at the delightful change for the better that had taken place in the personal appearance of his friend the charcoal-burner.

Yes,' he said, ' I'll come.'

So then the young man took him up very tenderly in his strong arms, and laid the little, tired head upon his breast and carried little Peter away.

Now it happened, strangely enough, that though both Susan Lepage and her husband sat watching by their child's bedside, they neither of them saw the young man with the calm face and shining hair, or heard a word he said. They only saw that the little boy opened his eyes suddenly and seemed to gaze at something with a kind of glad wonder, and that he smiled, and that his dear, little lips moved, and then that he stretched out his hands and laughed joyfully. After that he lay very still.

Susan Lepage waited a moment or two, then she rose and took a candle that stood on the oak chest near the bed's head. Shading it with her hand, she stooped down and looked closely at the child.

'Ah, my little one!' she cried.

She put the candle back again, and coming round

the foot of the bed, stood by Master Lepage, with her hand resting on his shoulder.

'My husband,' she said, 'our child will suffer no more. The dear Lord loved him and has called for him. A child has died on earth. A child is born in Paradise.'

There was a long silence. Master Lepage sat bolt upright with his arms hanging down at his sides—more as though he was standing before the general officer on parade, than sitting in the rush-bottomed chair in his own bedroom. The big tears ran down over his cheeks and fell from his moustache on to his blue blouse as thick as a summer shower.

'My wife,' he said slowly, 'our paths have joined at last—joined beside an open grave, but better there than nowhere. There shall be no more silence between us. The God whom you have served so faithfully in time will surely heal the smart of your sorrow. And perhaps He will condescend to listen to the prayers of a foolish, vainglorious, wrong-headed, old soldier, whom grief and repentance have humbled. Pardon me, my wife. I have been wrong and you right all along.

Lepage stood up, took her two hands in his, and kissed her.

'Ah, my dear, let us talk only of love and hope, not of pardon,' Susan Lepage answered gently.

She turned and looked at little Peter, still and smiling, with his round, black head resting so cosily on the white pillow.

'The autumn child has brought a blessing to the house,' she murmured.

'Ten thousand plagues!' broke out Master Lepage hoarsely. 'Twenty thousand cut-throat Prussians!—but I loved the little one.'

And is that the end of the story?

Well, yes, as far as a story can be said to have an end—most stories go on for ever, only we get tired or stupid and leave off reading them—if the story has an end, I say, I suppose this is it. Still there are just one or two little things I can mention which you might like to know. For instance, when next day Gustavus happened to pass the charcoal-burner's hut, he heard such a horrible barking, and yelling, that, though he was not of a very active or curious order of mind, he really had to go and see what was the matter. And on getting to the back of the hut he found Madelon, the sow, standing up on her hind legs in her sty, with her fore-feet resting on the rough, wooden door of it, her long, black snout high in the air, her floppety ears shaking, her great mouth wide open as she squealed aloud, and not a single scrap of food in her trough. This seemed to Gustavus such a singular thing, that though he had no great fancy for the society of the charcoal-burner, he thought he would just look inside the hut door, which stood half open. The snow had drifted in at it and lay thick on the mud floor within, there was no fire on the hearth, and the place was deathly chill. Yet Paqualin sat there sure enough, on a wooden bench, with his elbows on the table in front of him, and his head resting on his hands. His back was towards Gustavus. The cowherd did not quite like to go inside the hut somehow. He stood in the snow on the door-sill and called. At last he plucked up his courage, and going forward pulled at Paqualin's ragged sleeve.

'Umph,' said Gustavus, as he stumbled out again

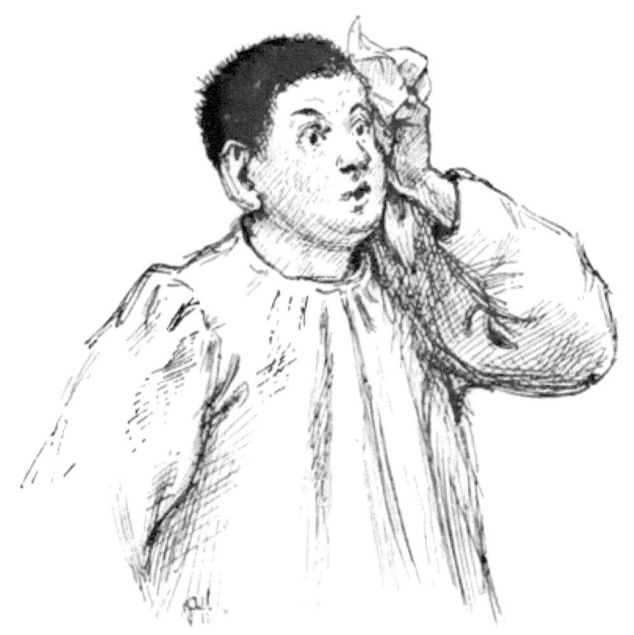

in a desperate hurry. He took off his hat and wiped his face round, for notwithstanding the frosty day, he felt quite uncomfortably warm.

'Here, I'll give you something, granny,' he called out to the sow. 'If you wait till your master brings it you'll wait a long time for your breakfast to-day. Bless me! but I shall have something to tell our Eliza this evening at supper that'll make her open her eyes!'

Antony has gone to serve his time in the army; and when his time is up and he comes back again to the old, wooden farm-house in the forest, I think it is very likely that the wish he wished in the dining-room of the Red Horse at Nullepart, when he shared the double filbert kernel with pretty Marie Georgeon, may really come true. Paul is apprenticed to an engineer in Paris, and lives among whirling machines in the great, crowded workshops; and his employers are much impressed with his ability and talent, and prophesy that he will make a name for himself some day. Cincinnatus is quite an old cat now, and his whiskers are almost white; but he still sits opposite the glowing wood fire in the kitchen, and blinks his big, yellow eyes and reflects on the superiority of cats to men. And Master Lepage still reads the history of the famous Roman Republic in the winter evenings, and takes off his spectacles and wipes them with his red pocket-handkerchief; but he rarely talks politics now, and never sits in the wine-shop, though on fine Sundays he often walks with his gentle, sweet-faced wife through the forest, and kneels humbly beside her in the church, and prays

God to guide and teach him, and forgive him all his sins.

And is this a true story?

Yes, as true as I can make it, and I have taken a good deal of pains.

But did it all really happen?

Ah! that is quite another question. For you will find as you grow older, that some of the very truest stories are those which, as most people in this world count happening, have never happened at all. And if you can't understand how that can be, I advise you, the first fine day, to ask your way to Nullepart and take the opinion of the Sacristan's cat upon the matter. He is a scholar, you know, so he is sure to be able to explain it.

THE END.

www.ingramcontent.com/pod-product-compliance
Lightning Source LLC
Chambersburg PA
CBHW030434190426
43202CB00036B/129